An Illustrated Guide to

Kendo

Solo

Training

A CLOSER LOOK AT THE SWORD SCROLL:
VOLUME 2

by

YAMAMOTO KANSUKE

TRANSLATED BY ERIC SHAHAN

An Illustrated Guide to Kendo Solo Training
A closer look at The Sword Scroll: Volume 2

Yamamoto Kansuke (1493-1561) was a hero of the century long Sengoku Era, roughly 1467-1600. Though partially blind and lame in one leg, Yamamoto Kansuke's prowess as a military strategist was legendary and his methods became a subject of study. In the Edo Era 1600-1868 several illustrated volumes attributed to him appeared, introducing his methods. These books explain his sword, spear and hidden weapon techniques.

The *A Closer Look at The Sword Scroll* series examines the many books attributed to Yamamoto Kansuke. While identical in parts, each book contains interesting variations that collectively add a great deal of information to those interested in traditional Japanese martial arts and military strategy. Originally presented as one volume, each book has been completely re-formatted and expanded, ideal for close study.

Volume 2 of *A Closer Look at The Sword Scroll* focuses on *An Illustrated Guide to Kendo Solo Training.* Both the date of publication and the artist are unclear. This book is notable for its excellent illustrations of early Kendo armor as well as mysterious techniques to fight Tengu, mythical winged mountain goblins. The "Solo Training" probably refers more to training without a teacher, rather than by yourself.

A Closer Look at the Sword Scroll Volumes 1 ~4

Volume 1
軍法兵法記釰術之巻 Gunpo Hyohoki Kenjutsu no Maki
(Published after 1546)

Way of the Sword and the Way of the Warrior: The Sword Scroll Gunpo Hyohoki Kenjutsu no Maki Zoho. Due to the opening remarks by Yamamoto Kansuke it was supposedly first published sometime after 1546.

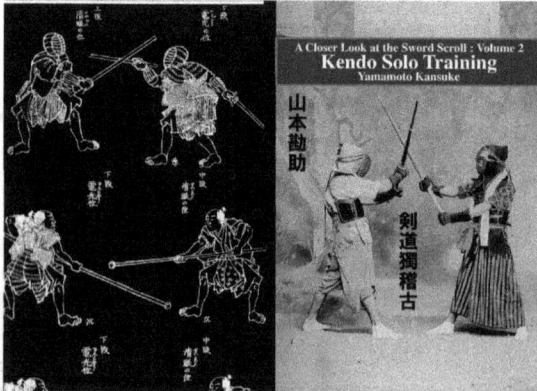

Volume 2
剣道獨稽古 Kendo Hitori Geiko (19th century)

An Illustrated Guide to Kendo Solo Training is notable for its excellent illustrations of early Kendo armor as well as mysterious techniques to fight Tengu, mythical winged mountain goblins.

Volume 3

● 武術早學 Bujutsu Haya Manabi
A Quick Guide to Martial Arts
19th Century

This edition is notable for two additional sections showing boxing and wood staff techniques, which do not appear in any other version.

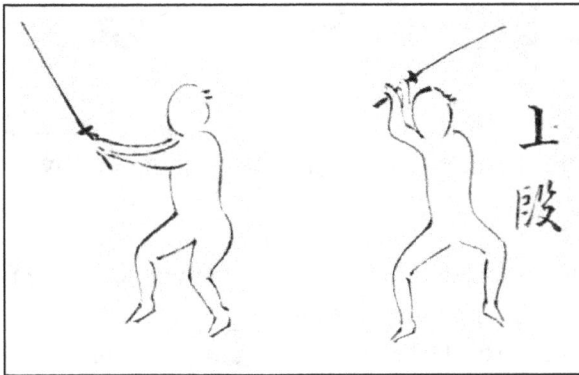

Volume 4
軍事参考軍法兵法記：楠正成秘書
Kusonogi Masashige Hissho Gunji Sanko Gunpo Heiho Ki
Kusonogi Masashige's Secret Martial Arts Scroll on Military Strategy and Sword Fighting

   This version is by Wakichi Sakurai has a definitive publication date of 1914. Sakurai draws parallels between Yamamoto Kansuke and the 14th century warlord Kusunoki Masashige.楠木正成 (1294 –1336) He is held up as the ideal Samurai for his service to his lord.

Yamamoto Kansuke 山本勘助

山本勘助軍配團 *Yamamoto Kansuke Gunpaiden.*
Yamamoto Kansuke (getting his eye gouged out by a wild boar whilst hunting) Edo Era book

Yamamoto Kansuke (1493-1561)whose given name is variously written as 勘助、 勘介 or 菅助 was born at the end of the late 15th or early 16th Century and died at the fourth Kawanakajima battle in 1561. His woodpecker strategy, similar to the pincer movement, is widely praised as an example of excellent military tactics. Unfortunately he believed his woodpecker strategy to be a failure so he attempted to regain his honor by charging into the enemy ranks, being killed in action.

Kansuke is mainly famous for his *Heiho Ogisho* 兵法奥義書, a book that is contained within the *Koyo Gunkan* 甲陽軍鑑. Some elements of the Heiho Ogisho are found within the Sword Scroll as well, though they differ somewhat in length and format.

Cover of Kendo Hitori Keiko : Solo Kendo Training

The first illustrations in this book show the warrior Yoshitsune training sword fighting in the forest. Behind him, the ghostly image of a Tengu, a mountain goblin is instructing him. Yoshitsune has tied a rope to a stick and hung it from a tree and is using it as a training device. Later books on Kendo credit Yoshitsune with inventing this training method.

Illustration of Yoshitsune fighting Benkei by Utagawa Hiroshige 1835

Minamoto no Yoshitsune 源義経 (1159-89) was a Samurai whose exploits, both real and legendary are recorded in works such as the Tale of the Heike and The Annals of Yoshitsune. They are the source of many Noh, Kabuki and Joruri puppet plays as well. Regarding martial arts one of his most memorable episodes is how he was placed in Kuramadera Temple near Kyoto when he was a youth. While he studied at the temple during the day, at night he was instructed by Tengu, who taught him sword fighting and other martial arts. He later used the leaping style of the Tengu to defeat the warrior-monk Benkei (illustration above.)

This training method can be found in many martial arts books from the Edo through the early Showa eras, roughly 1600-1930.

Below is an illustration from *The Physical Educator's Essential Guide to Martial Arts Demonstration*s 體育演武必携 1896 by Sumimoto Sanemichi 隅元實道. The text is translated on the right:

七　此の釣球は傳に曰く、双腕上下。擴張胸膈。劍法素養。亦在其中と。

一は牛若の鞍馬山に於ける修業も是れなりしと云ふ。先づ両手を伸べ、漸く刀尖の屆く位に高く釣り、圓陣より出て〻仰視脊伸びし繼け擊つ。乃ち競爭心を起し胸膈を擴げ劍法の素養を得る。請ふ旃れを勉め。

（釣球は革にて包む）

第二圖

This hanging training ball comes with the following instructions: Both arms go up and down, the chest fully expands and contracts, by doing so it develops your Kenpo, sword skill.

This method originated with Yoshitsune when he was a youth known as Young Bull, training on Mount Kurama.

First extend both arms while holding your sword. Hang the ball just at the point the tip of your sword can touch. Keeping you gaze upward swing your sword (probably a wooden one) in an arc, continuously striking it. This will develop your fighting spirit and help expand your chest, thereby developing your sword technique.

The ball can be covered with leather.

1. Yoshitsune riding on the Tengu to take his Fencing Lessons at Kurama Yama.

天狗に乗って鞍馬に剣道を習いに行く義経
Yoshitsune riding on the Tengu to take his Fencing Lessons at Kurama Yama 1880 by Edward James (1830-1906)

Layout

Each page in this book has pictures of two combatants, as shown above. They are shown in different Stance, or stances, divided into three broad categories Jodan, Chudan and Gedan. Jodan is with the sword or spear held at or above head level, Chudan is around waist level and Gedan has the handle of the sword at waist level with the point facing the ground.

In addtion to the broad category of Jodan, Chudan and Gedan there is a sub-name for each illustration and a notation about foot positioning. The sub-names are quite poetic and therefore hard to translate accurately without being directly involved in this school of martial arts, therefore the translations should be considered approxamate. The notation regarding foot postitioning is either "floating foot" or "planted foot" which, based on the illustrations indicates the "ball of your foot off the ground" for the former and "foot flat on the ground" in the latter. It Some of the illustrations also contain additional information of varying lenghts.

For the most part each page will be presented as it was in the orininal book then each Stance will be isolated and enlarged, with the information on the page translated above. This is shown on the following page.

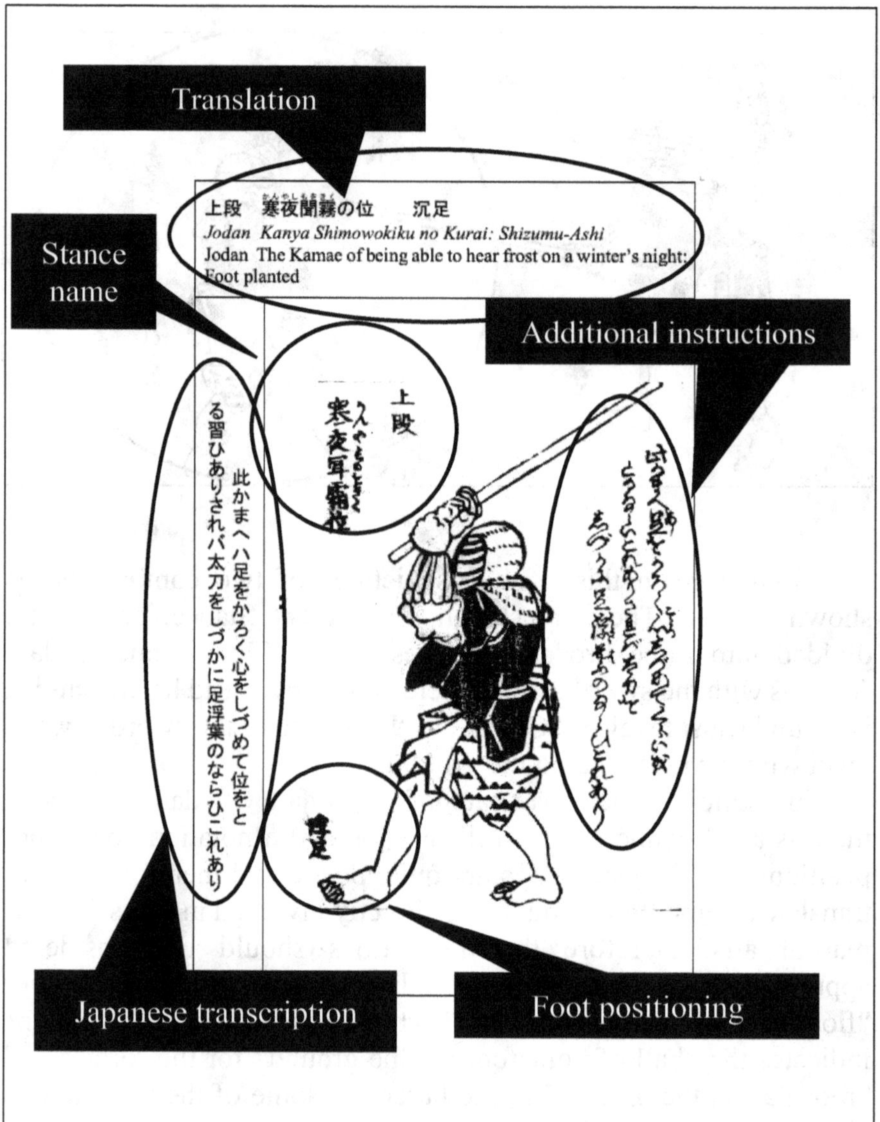
Translation
上段　寒夜聞霜の位　　沈足
Jodan Kanya Shimowokiku no Kurai: Shizumu-Ashi
Jodan The Kamae of being able to hear frost on a winter's night: Foot planted
Stance name
Additional instructions
上段
此かまへハ足をかろく心をしづめて位をとる習ひありされバ太刀をしづかに足浮葉のならひこれあり
Japanese transcription
Foot positioning

A closer look at The Sword Scroll: Volume 2
An Illustrated Guide to Kendo Solo Training

by
YAMAMOTO KANSUKE

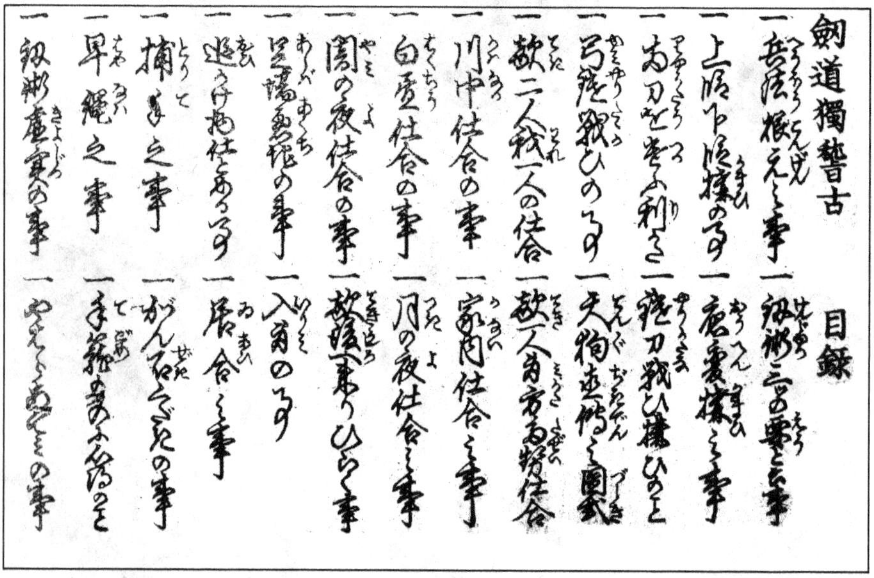

剣道獨習古　　目録

一　兵法根えと事　　　　　　一　段砌ニ四の事と之事
一　上段下段搆のす　　　　　一　店衾密と之事
一　刀をぬく利さ　　　　　　一　沱刀戦ハ捷ひのこと
一　弓箭戦ひのこと　　　　　一　天狗走飛の圖繪
一　敵二人我一人の仕合　　　一　敵人身方る勝仕合
一　川中仕合の事　　　　　　一　家内仕合と事
一　白昼仕合の事　　　　　　一　月の夜仕合と事
一　星屈あ梢の事　　　　　　一　入身のす
一　逃うけ拘仕あるす　　　　一　居合と事
一　捕きと事　　　　　　　　一　がんぞくぞんの事
一　早縄之事　　　　　　　　一　手縛あふ治のこ
一　級砌産實の事　　　　　　一　やえくらあとこの事

Table of Contents

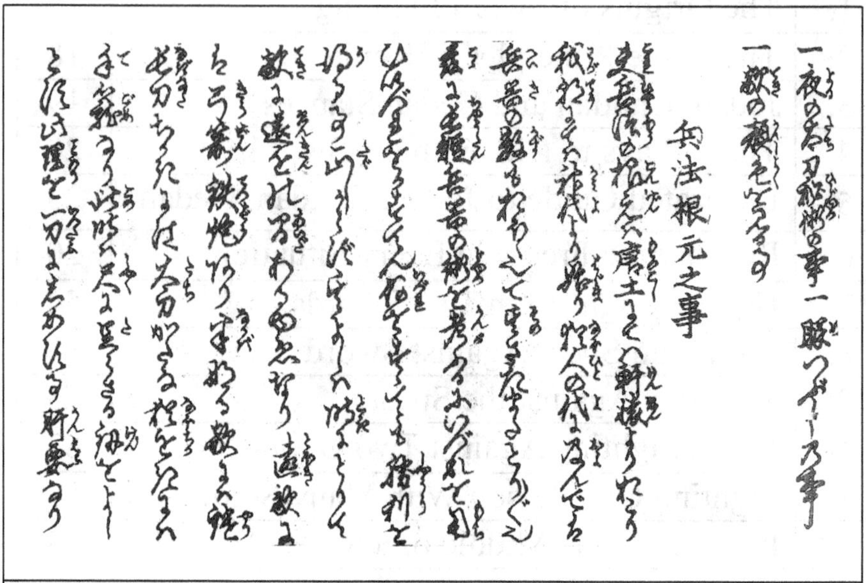

兵法根元之事
もろこし

夫兵法の根元ハ唐土にては軒轅よりおこり
我朝にては神代より始り、猶人の代に及んでは

兵器の数もおほくなりて其てさた、
多く

またとりどりなり

茲に長短兵器の術を考ふるにいづれを用
いづれ

ひ、いづれをかすてん、何をすてても勝利を
由

得る事正しからず其よしは時にとりて

敵に遠近の間あるゆゑなり　と遠敵に
きゅうせん

は弓箭鉄炮なり　半なる敵には鑓
なかば

長刀ちかきには太刀かたな、猶近きには
なぎなた　　　　た　　　　なおちか

手籠なり此時は尺に足らざる剣をよし
てごめ　この　　　　　　　　　　　　　　ことわり

とす時　理　を一刀にしめする肝要なり

一夜の名刀秘術の事一眠つけゐる事
一敵の観えたゐる事

兵法根元之事

(Left) Ken-en 軒轅 also known as the Yellow Emperor
(Right) Chiyou 蚩尤 the rival of Ken-en

The Origins of Sword Fighting

Military strategy (sword fighting) originated with Ken-en, also known as the Yellow Emperor of China (2510-2448 BC.) In our own country it began in the age of the gods and has continued on into the age of men. The kinds of weapons in use have increased in number and variation. The way in which long and short weapons are utilized should be considered. Each has its strong point, and there is a time to abandon each in order to achieve victory.

This all depends on your distance from the enemy. Arrows and rifles for long distances, closer then Yari and Naginata. When closer use the Tachi. If the fight goes to Tegome, or hand to hand, you should make use of a blade shorter than one Shaku, or 30 centimeters.

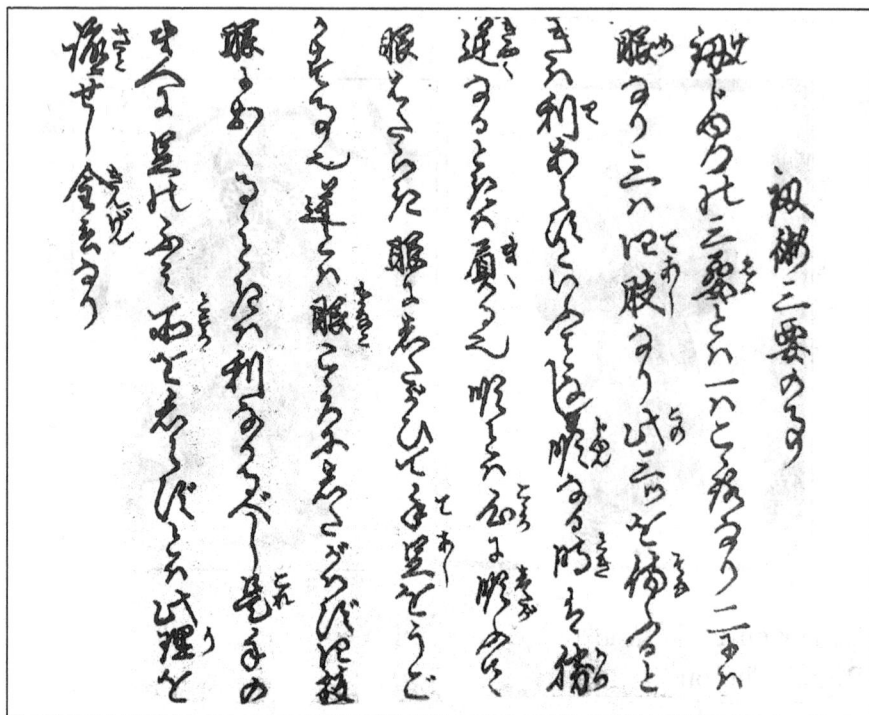

釼術三要のこと
Kenjutsu San Kaname no Koto
Three Principals of Kenjutsu

There are three basic principles in Kenjutsu. One is the spirit. The second is the eye. The third comprises the feet and hands. If these three are all in accordance/balance then you will achieve victory. If they are confused then you will be defeated. In accordance means that the spirit, the mind, is communicating to the eyes correctly. It means the eyes are correctly directing the feet and hands. In confusion means the eyes do not move in accordance with the spirit.

Having eyes delay the movement of the limbs of the body will give a poor result. However, if these three elements are activated correctly and in unison the result will be positive. This is exactly the same as the condition whereby having moved the hands you are not sure of where to put your feet.

上段中段構の事
Jodan, Chudan and Gedan Stances

When going into Stance with a sword, know that Jodan, Chudan and Gedan are the only Stance. This is the first lesson of Kenjutsu. Further, when studying and adapting your body to these Stance having Yokoshimana Kokoro 邪な心 or no evil in your heart is best.

A person came to me once and said "In Kenjutsu the shape changes depending on the enemy. It follow then that there is only one Kimeru 極める, or only one rule, in Kenjutsu. What do you think of this?

The response was, "Having control over your spirit is certainly a Kimeru 極める. And having learned the three principals, or Kaname 要, you can consider yourself to have achieved this state. Having achieved this state of Shigoku 至極, or the ultimate, there is really nothing more to be said. For that reason, the way in which the arms and legs are bent should be studied extensively.

19

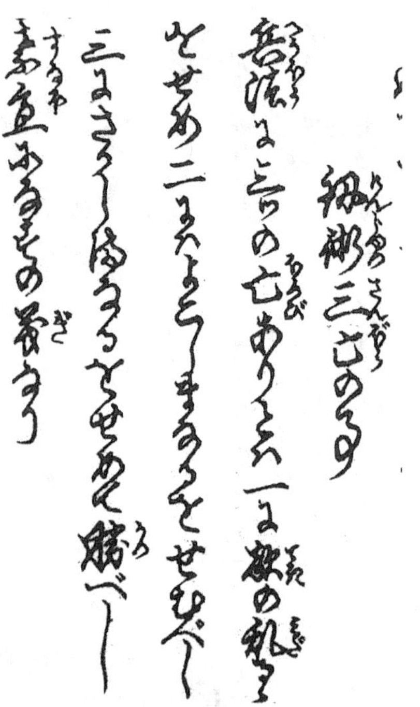

剣術三亡の事

兵法に三つの亡（ほろび）ありとは一に敵の乱るるをせめ、二にはよこしまなるをせめむべし、三にはさかしまなるをせめて勝べし。素直になれの義なり

剣術三亡の事
Kenjutsu Sanbo no Koto
Three Ways to Kill With the Sword

Kenjutsu, the art of the sword, teaches three ways to kill. The first is to confuse or distract the enemy, the second is to deceive them, and the third is attack in an unexpected manner.

20

天文十五年丙午皐月

甲陽　山本道鬼齋

晴幸

What I said about Stance also applies to Yari (spear) and Naginata (halberd.) Further, within Jodan Stance there lies Jo-upper, Chu-middle and Ge-lower. Also within Chudan Stance there lies Jo-upper, Chu-middle and Ge-lower. All together there are thirty-three versions. It is said that Kenjutsu contains and endless procession of Sen-pen-ban-ka 千変万化 or a thousand changes and ten thousand variations.

However there are no Stance other than those I mentioned, Jodan, Chudan and Gedan. Those starting on the path of the sword should study these three stances. Learning to cut as soon as a chance presents itself and respond to any Henka, or variation, is of the upmost importance.

Fifteenth year of Tenbun May First 1546
Yamamoto Dokisai (Dokisai is his Buddhist name) Kansuke Haruyuki

This is Yamamoto Kansuke's stylized "Kao" signature. It is derived from the Kanji for "Suke" in Kansuke 助.

21

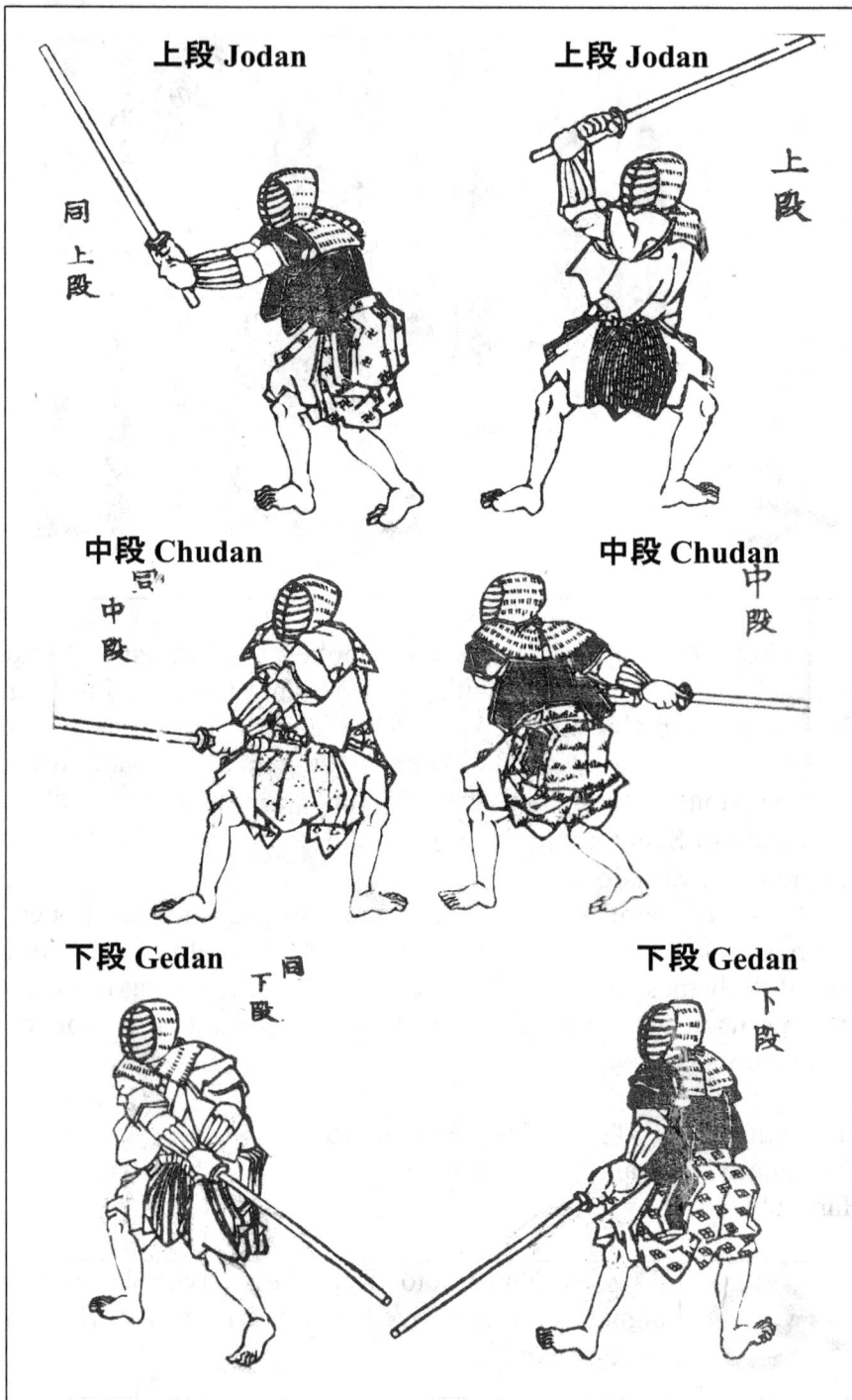

上段 Jodan

上段 Jodan

同上段

上段

中段 Chudan

中段 Chudan

中段

中段

下段 Gedan

下段 Gedan

同下段

下段

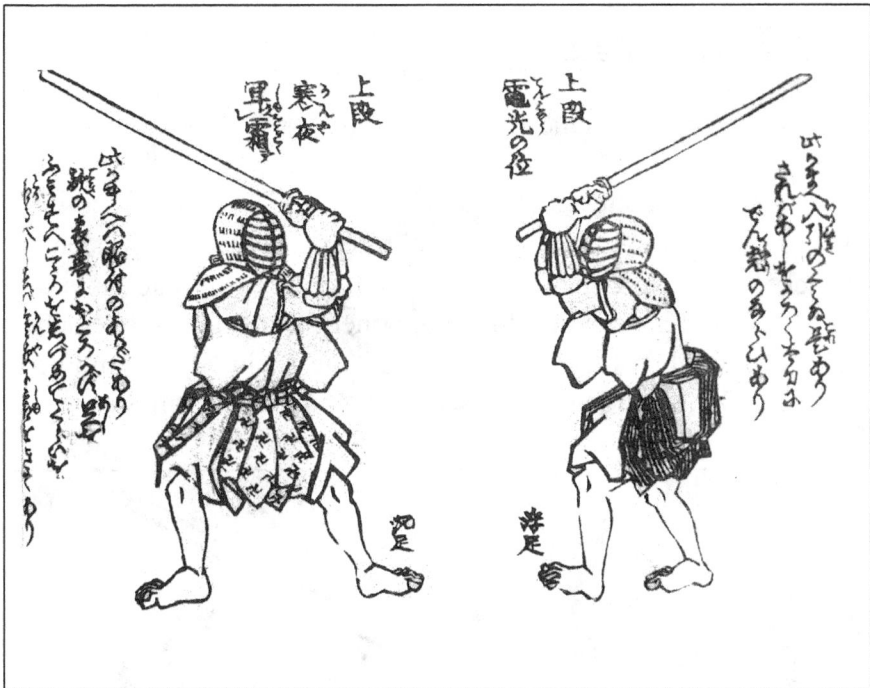

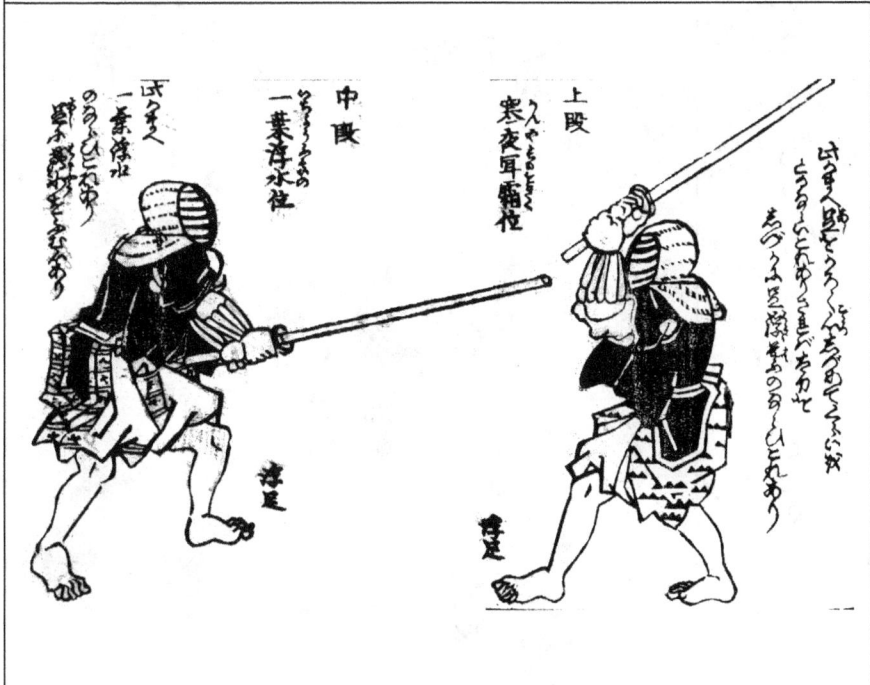

上段電光の位　浮足

Jodan : Denko no Kurai : Uki-ashi

Jodan : Lightning Stance : Floating foot

This Kamae is about the Ma-ai 間合い or distancing of Irimi 入身, or entering into an ideal space in response to the opponent's attack or movement, and Hikimi 引身, or drawing back into an ideal position in response to the opponent's attack or movement. The foot is lightly touching the ground, the Tachi 太刀 is imbibed with the Denko Hiden, or the secret teaching of lightning.

上段
電光の位

ひくまえ入引のくゐ墨あり
されがめせうろくを刀み
どん我のゐゑとひめり

上段電光の位　浮足

此かまえ入引の位これありされバ足をか
ろく、太刀に電光の習ひあり

浮足

上段　寒夜聞霧の位　　沈足

Jodan : Kanya Shimowokiku no Kurai: Shizumu-Ashi

Jodan : The Kamae of being able to hear frost on a winter's night: Planted Foot

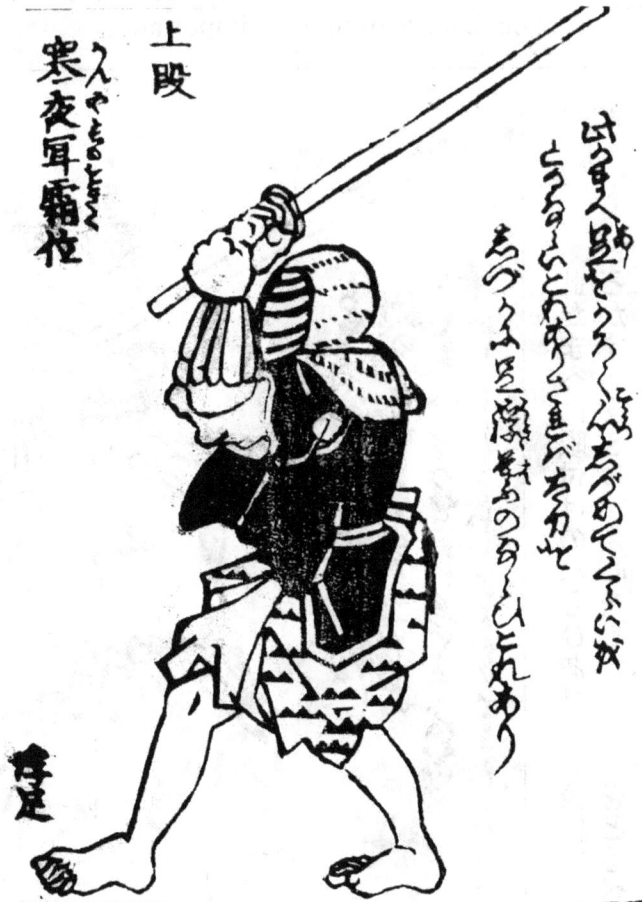

此かまへ八足をかろく心をしづめて位をとる習ひありされバ太刀をしづかに足浮葉のならひこれあり

上段　寒夜聞霧の位　沈足

Jodan : Kanya Shimowokiku no Kurai: Shizumu-Ashi

Jodan : The stance of being able to hear frost crack on a winter's night : Floating foot

The secret teaching of this stance is to stay light on your feet and calm your spirit. Having done that draw the Tachi and position it silently. The feet should be kept as light as a leaf floating on water. The feet are of upmost importance.

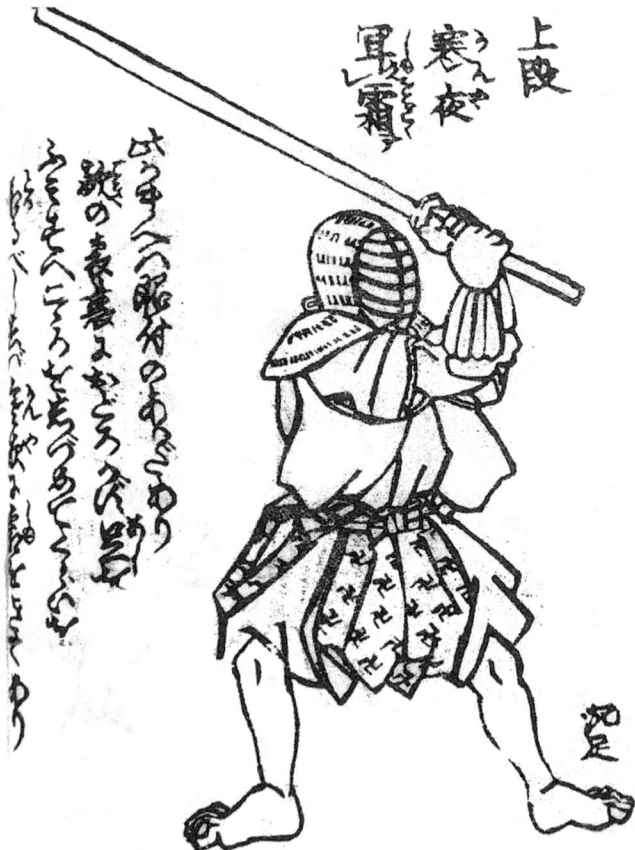

此かまへに眼付けのならひあり敵の表裏におどろかず足をふみすえ心をしづめて位をとるべし

中段　一葉浮水の位　浮足
Chudan : Ichi-e Fusui no Kurai : Uki-Ashi
Chudan : Leaf floating upon water Stance: Planted Foot

The meaning of this stance is to position yourself like a leaf floating upon water. The feeling should be as if the feet are stepping on ice.

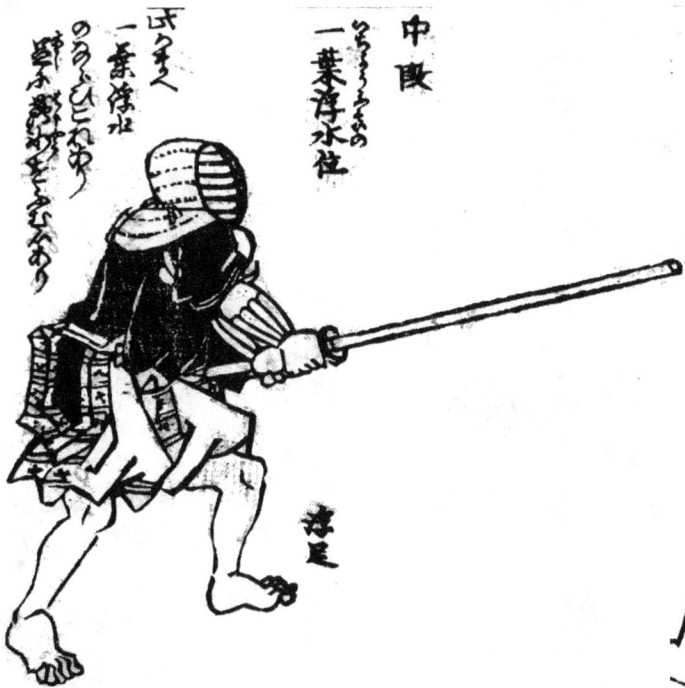

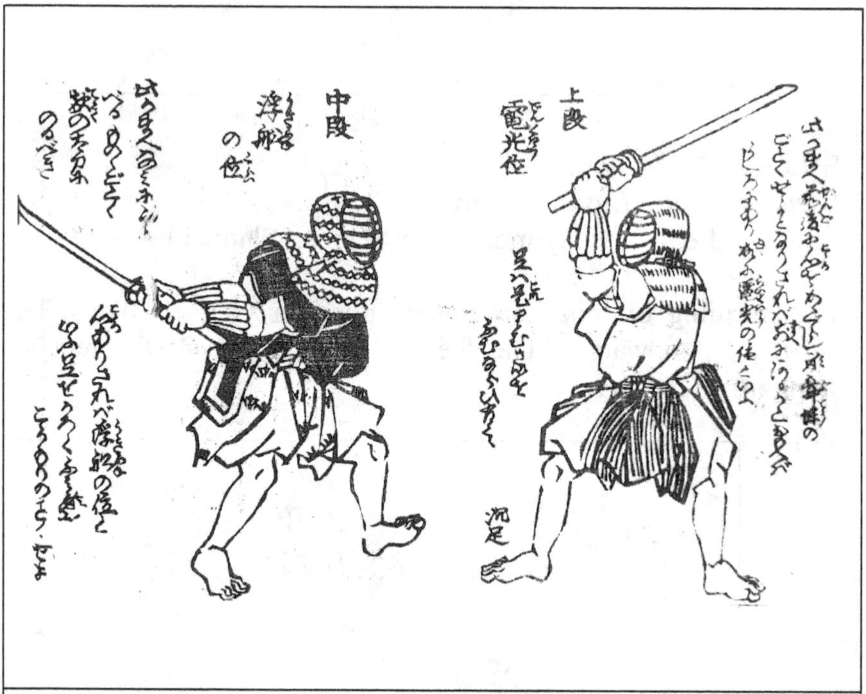
上段
電光位
中段
浮舟の位

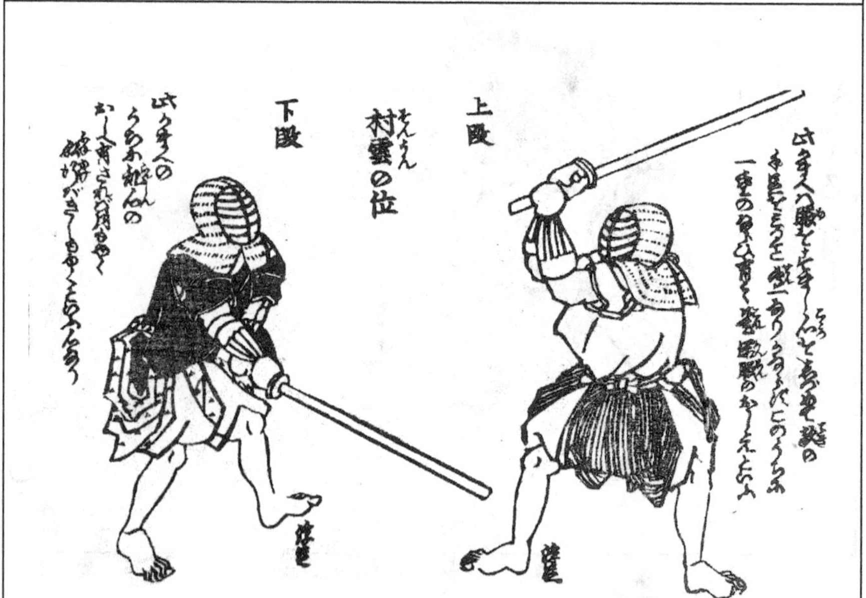
上段
村雲の位
下段

上段　電光の位　沈足

Jodan : Denko no Kurai : Shizumu-Ashi
Jodan : Lightning Stance : Planted Foot

As you alternate switching your feet out your center of gravity moves back to front. For this stance you should concentrate on both what is in front of you as well as what is behind you. Your body should move lightly, dancing like a butterfly. If done in this fashion, from the opponent's point of view, it will seem to him as if you are in front of him when suddenly you have circled around behind him. Therefore you are extremely hard to corner. This is the stance known as Denko no Kurai, the Lightning Stance.

中段　浮船の位　浮足

Chudan Fusen no Kurai : Uki-Ashi

Chudan : The Floating Boat Stance : Floating Foot.

The feeling of this stance is of watching the opponent's Tachi while you float like an object going up and down waves. That is why this Stance is called Fusen no Kurai, the Floating Boat Stance. The feet are touching lightly and the bodyweight should be placed as lightly as a feather

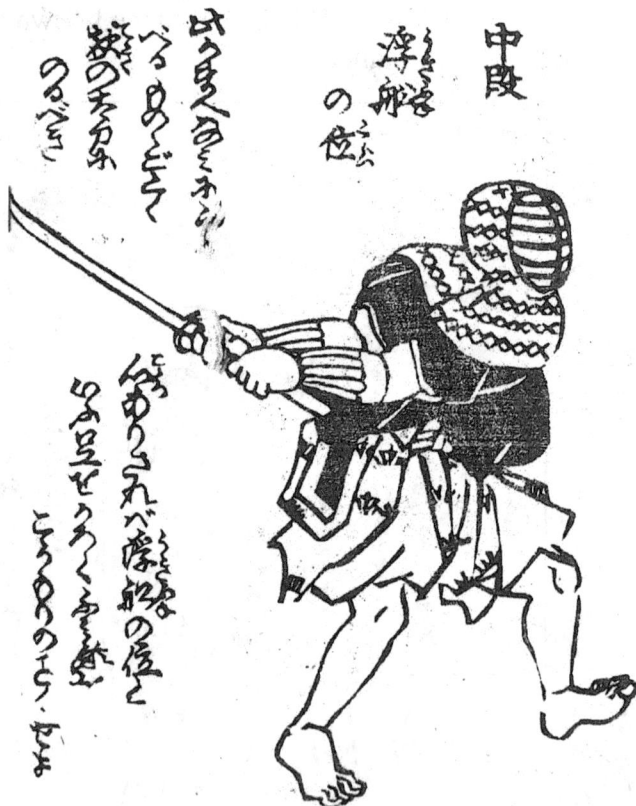

上段　村雲の位　沈足

Jodan : Sonun no Kurai : Shizumu-Ashi
Jodan : Cloudy Village Stance : Planted foot

Keep the feet together and impart a sense of sleepiness. The meaning of this stance is to clear your vision, calm your spirit and focus everything on the opponent's strategy. By doing this you will invariably discern something.

上段

此かまへ八眼をすまし心をしづめて敵の手位をみる事専一なり、必此内に一重のならひ有之是を閑眠のおしへといふ

此ま〳〵眼をすます〳〵と志づめ 敵の手位をよくみるに 発一声に志て その内より一重の術八 すみやかに発歐歐のおしへとなふ

下段 村雲の位　浮足

Gedan : Sonun no Kurai : Uki-Ashi

Gedan : Cloudy Village Stance : Floating Foot

There is nothing in this stance that teaches that the spirit is in tumult. Like windblown clouds, across the face of the moon your spirit should be like a boat slowly being swept up onto the beach.

Note: The Kanji for Cloudy Village Stance are sometimes written as Sonun no Kurai and sometimes as Murakumo.

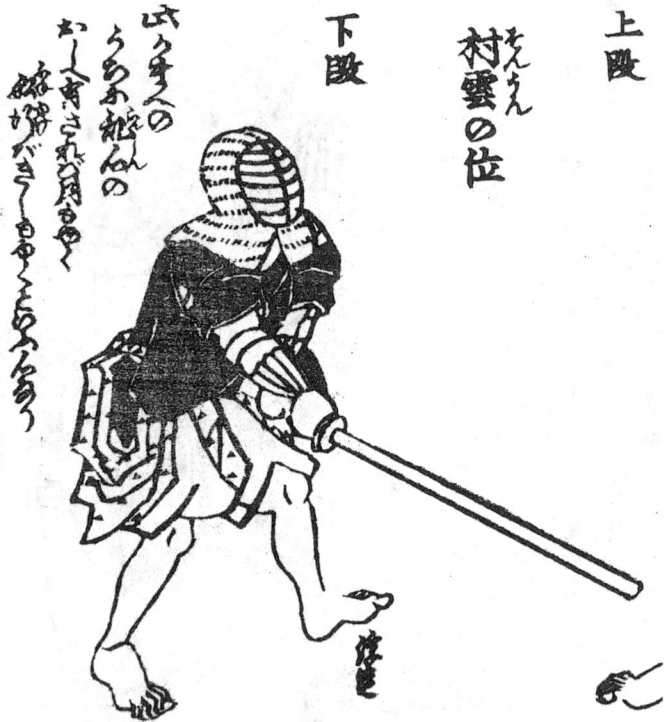

上段

そ ゑ ん
村雲の位

下段

此ノ手ノの
うらふ船んの
おゝ寄さ気月もゆく
姚ゆがざ〜もゆくとゆふ〜

此かまへのうちに乱心のおしへ有、されバ
風に雲の行ごとく雲ゆけば月もゆく船ゆけ
ばきしもゆくといふ心なり

32

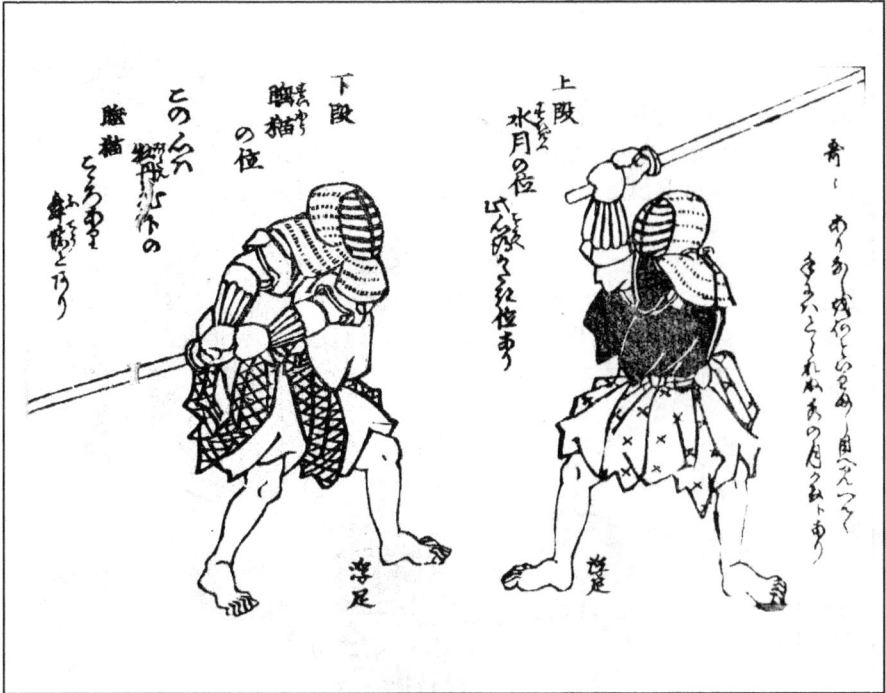

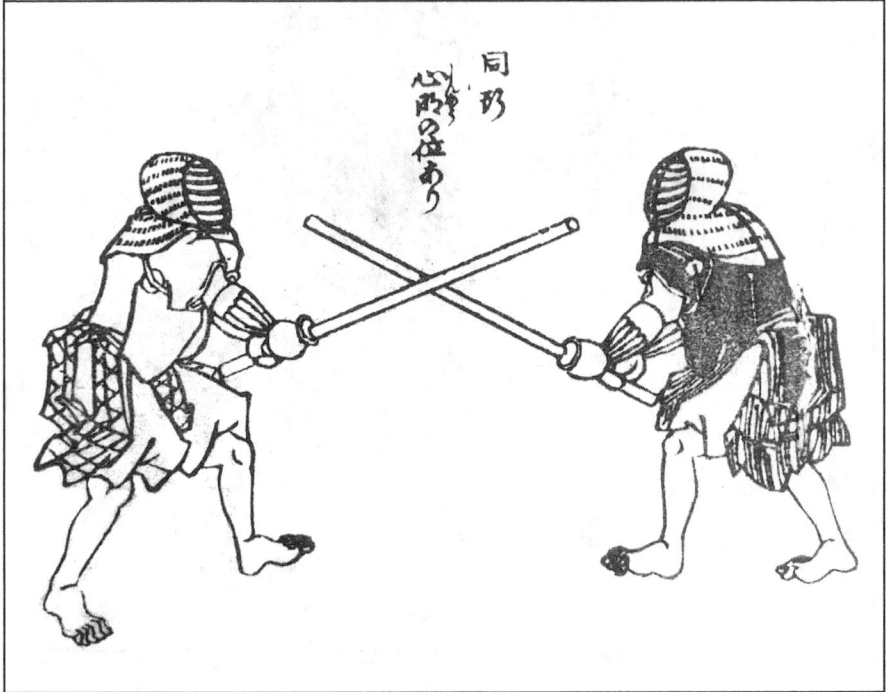

33

上段　水月の位　浮足

Jodan : Suigetsu no Kurai : Uki-Ashi

Jodan : Moon Reflected on Water Stance : Floating Foot

There is a song that talks of how this is a difficult stance to adopt. It is said that what is there is not there. The water that pools in one hand shows a different moon from the one above.

この心得かたき位なり歌に云う、ありなしを何といはまし月にミえて手にハしられぬ水の月かなとあり

下段　睡猫の位　浮足

Gedan : Suibyou no Kurai : Uki-Ashi

Gedan : Sleeping Cat Stance : Floating Foot

The way of thinking about this stance is a sleeping cat below a Botan flower with a dancing butterfly above.

この心牡丹花下の睡猫心あり舞蝶とあり

同段　　心妙の位あり

Do-Stance : Shinmyo no Kurai

Same Stance: Mysterious Heart Stance

There is a Kuden, Orally Transmitted Lesson

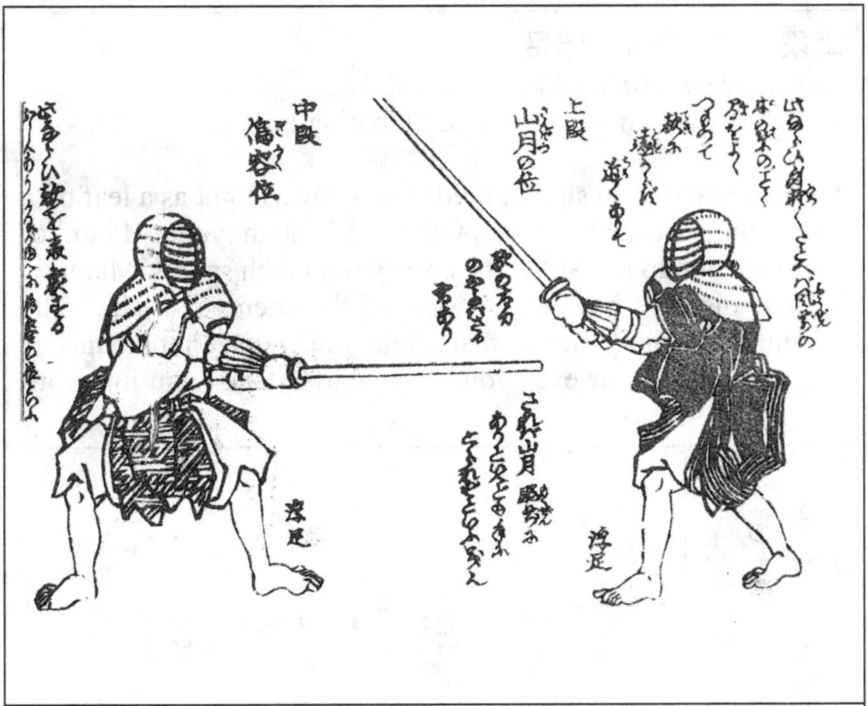
上段
山月の位
中段
偽容位

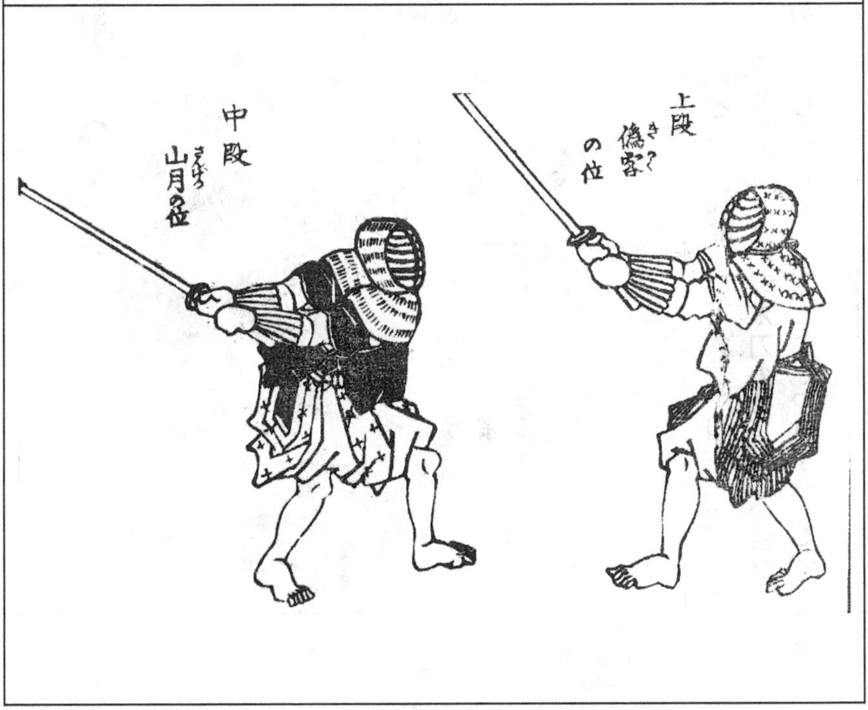
上段
偽容の位
中段
山月の位

上段　山月の位　浮足

Jodan : Sangetsu no Kurai : Uki-Ashi

Jodan : Mountain Moon Stance : Floating Foot

For this Stance you should hold your body as light as a leaf on a tree being brushed by the wind.　Maintain your Ma-ai, or distance, but do not allow the enemy too much space.　Maintain a close distance but out of range of the enemy's Tachi.　The meaning of this Stance is that while you can see mountains or the moon with your eyes you are unable to take them into your hand.

此ならひ身軽くたとへバ風前の木の葉の如く。間をよくつもって敵にからすくありて敵の太刀の及バざる習ひありされバ山月眼前にありといへども手にしられずといふ語あり

中段　偽客の位　浮足

Chudan : Gikaku no Kurai : Uki Ashi

Chudan : False Guest Stance : Floating Foot

This Stance contains teachings on how to control the Hyori, or Obverse and Reverse, of the opponent. Both his true and hidden intent. For that reason it is known as Gikaku.

(Left) 中段山月の位 Chudan : *Sangetsu no Kurai*
Chudan : Mountain Moon Stance

(Right) 上段偽客の位 *Jodan : Gikaku no Kurai*
Jodan : False Guest Stance

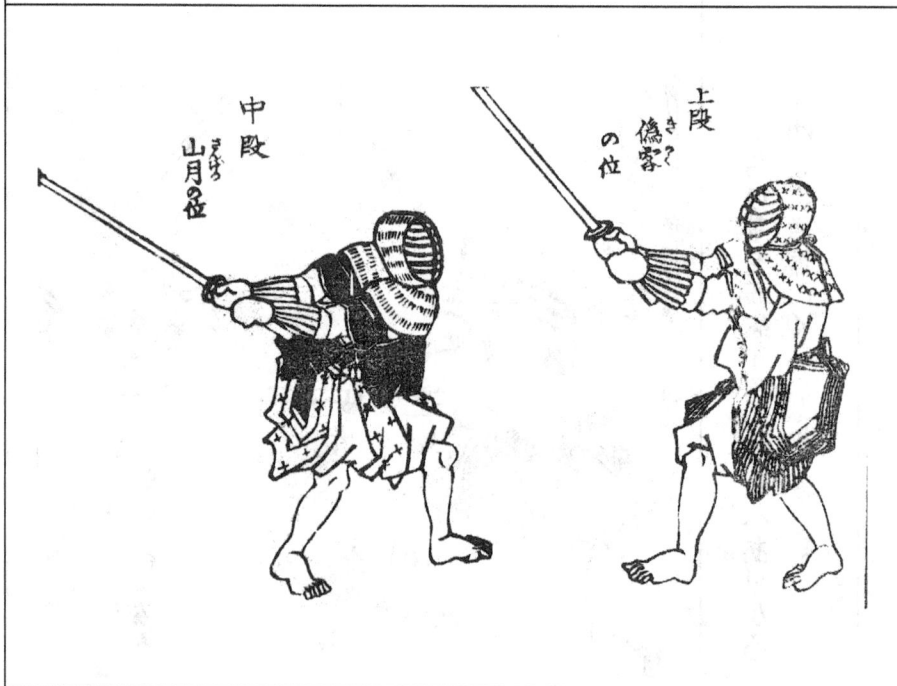

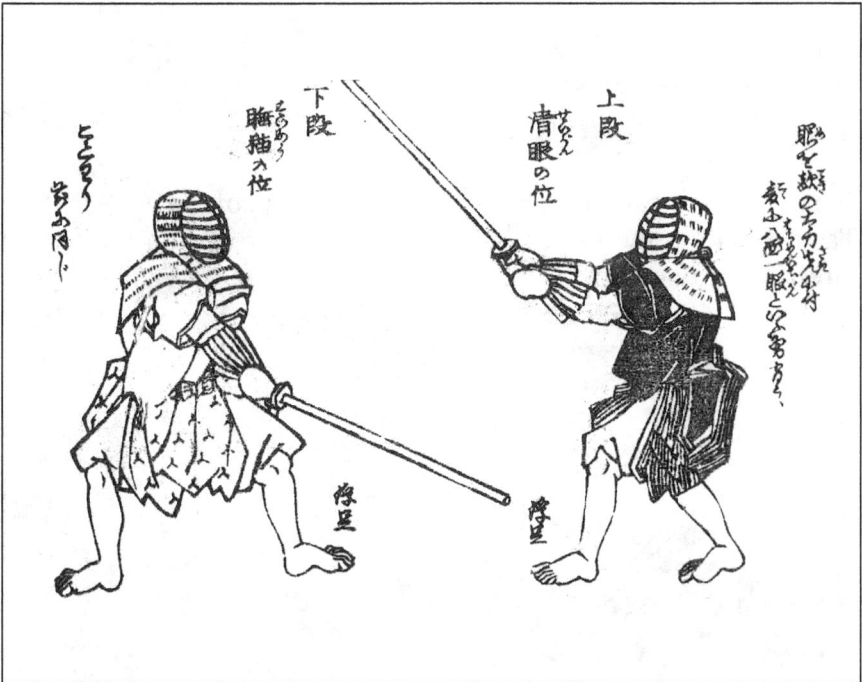

上段　清眼の位　浮足

Jodan Seigan no Kurai Uki-Ashi

Jodan : Seigan Stance: Floating foot

Here you are meant to keep your eye on the end of the opponent's Tachi while at the same time keep your other eye on the eight directions around you.

眼を敵の太刀先につけ八面一眼といふ習あり
ことわりまへにあり

下段　睡猫の位　浮足

Gedan Suibyo no Kurai Uki-Ashi

Gedan: Sleeping Cat Stance : Floating Foot

Explanation is the same as before

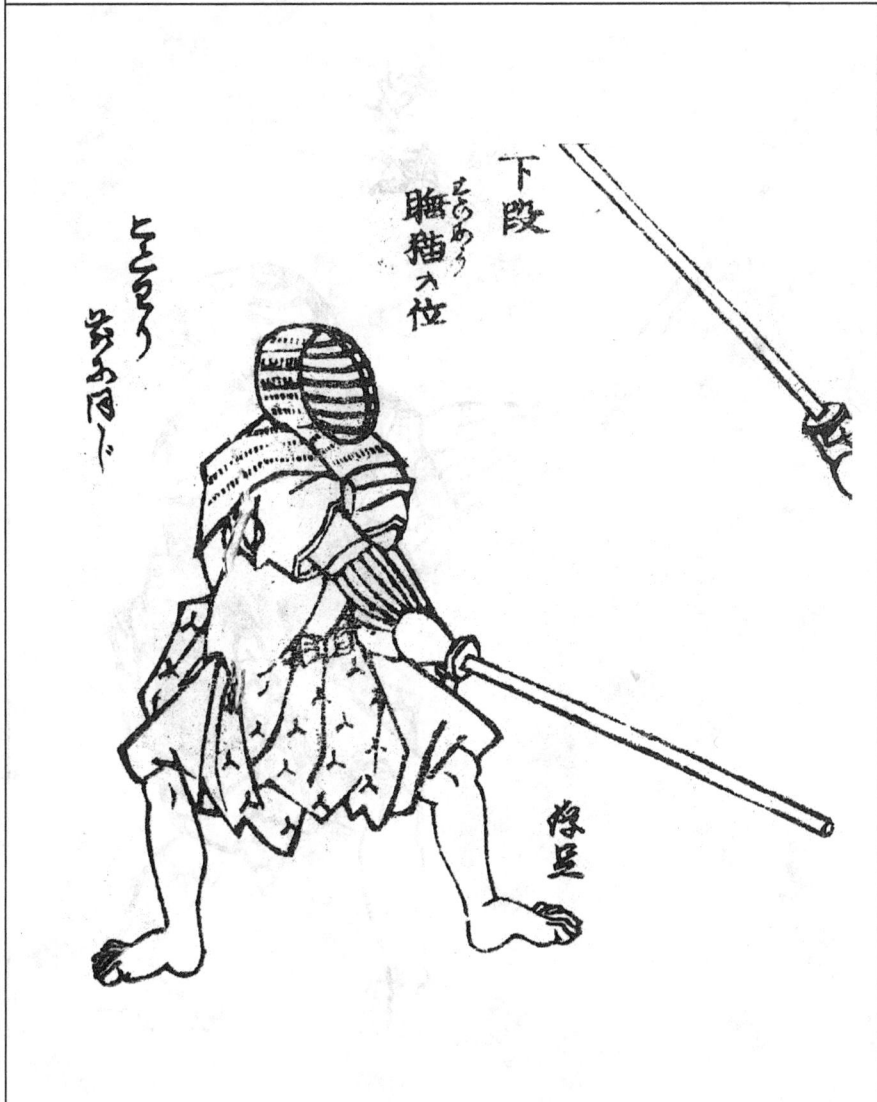

寒夜聞霧の位　浮

Kanyashimo wo Kiku no Kurai Uki-Ashi

Floating foot : The stance of being able to hear frost crack on a winter's night : Floating Foot.

Note: I presume this is Jodan, however there is no notation.

入引の位　浮

ことわり電光の位に 爪（つぶさ）に書くしるし侯也

Nyuin no Kurai Uki-Ashi

Moving In and Out Stance : Floating Foot

The explanation for this is the same as for Denko no Kurai.
Note: I presume this is Gedan, however there is no notation.

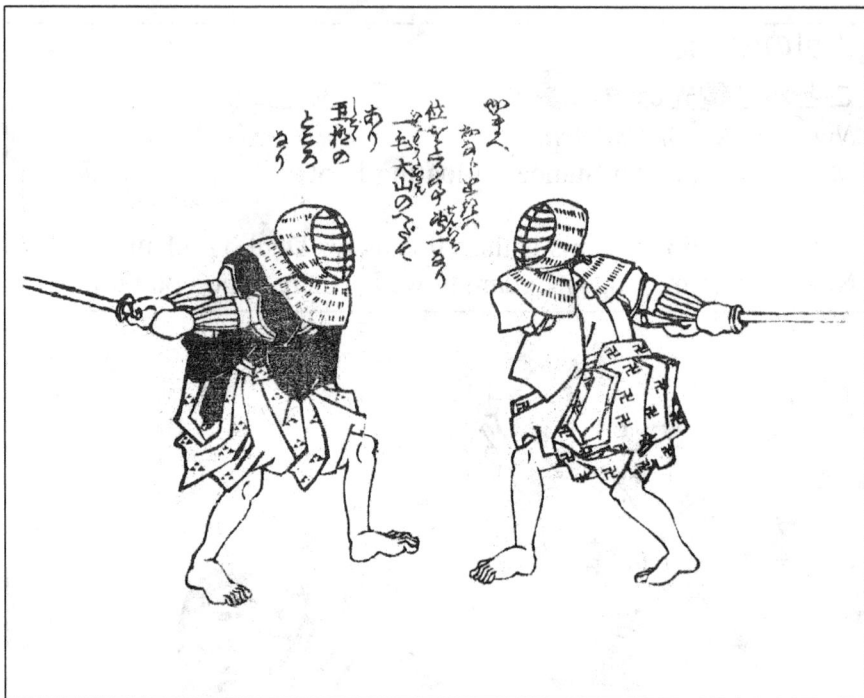

KENDO SOLO TRAINING・剣道獨稽古

かまへおなしときハ
位をとること専一なり
一毛火山のへだて有至極の所也

When both you and the opponent are in the same stance, the battle is over positioning. The feeling is of a mountain being squeezed inward by two opposing warriors. An extreme feeling.

中段　清眼の位　浮ことわりまへにあり
水月の位

(Right) *Chudan : Seigan no Kurai*
Chudan: Clear-eyed Stance
The explanation is as before. The foot is floating Uki Ashi style.

(Left) *Suigetsu no Kurai*
Moon Reflected on Water Stance

47

(Right) 中段 清眼の位 浮 *Chudan : Seigan no Kurai : Uki-Ashi*
Chudan : Clear-eyed Stance : Floating foot
ことわりまへにあ Explanation is as before.

(Left) 下段 村雲の位 浮 *Gedan : Murakumo no Kurai : Uki-Ashi*
Gedan: Cloudy Village Stance : Floating foot

(Right) 中段清眼の位浮足 *Chudan : Seigan no Kurai : Uki-Ashi*
Chudan : Clear-eyed Stance : Floating foot
ことわりまへにあり　Explanation is as before.

(Left) 下段　村雲の位 Gedan : Murakumo no Kurai
Gedan :

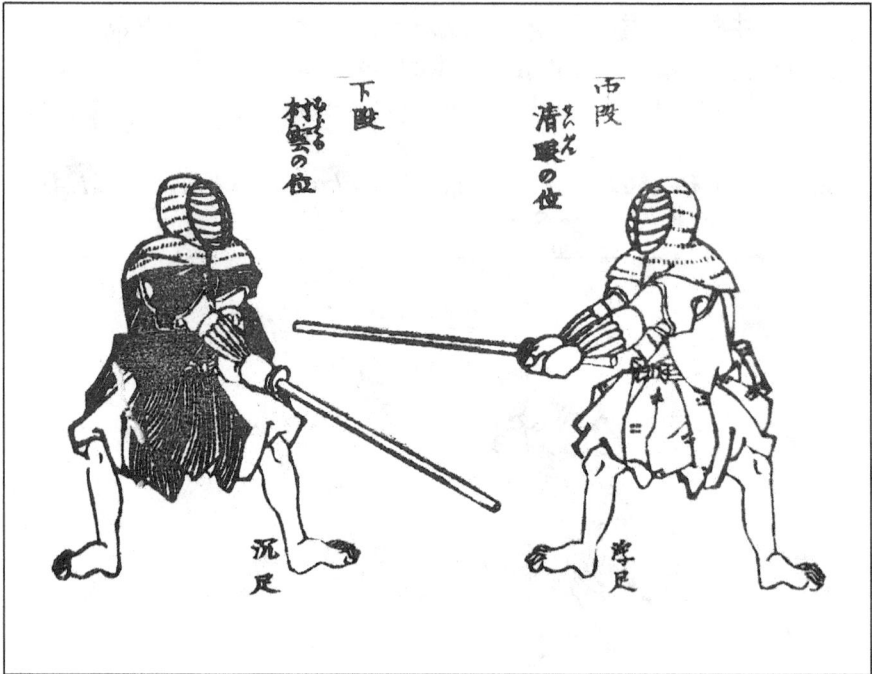

(Right)
中段 清眼の位浮足 *Chudan : Seigan no Kurai : Uki-Ashi*
Chudan : Clear-eyed Stance : Floating foot

(Left)
下段 村雲の位沉 *Gedan : Murakumo no Kurai :Shizumu-Ashi*
Gedan : Cloudy Village Stance : Planted foot

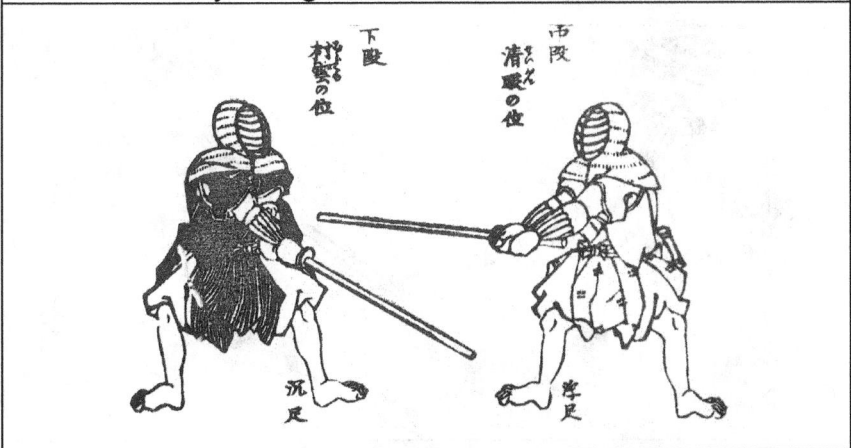

(Right)
中段 清眼の位沉 *Chudan : Seigan no Kurai : Shizumu-Ashi*
Chudan : Clear-eyed Stance : Planted Foot

(Left)
下段　村雲の位浮足 *Gedan : Murakumo no Kurai : Uki-Ashi*
Gedan : Cloudy Village Stance : Floating Foot

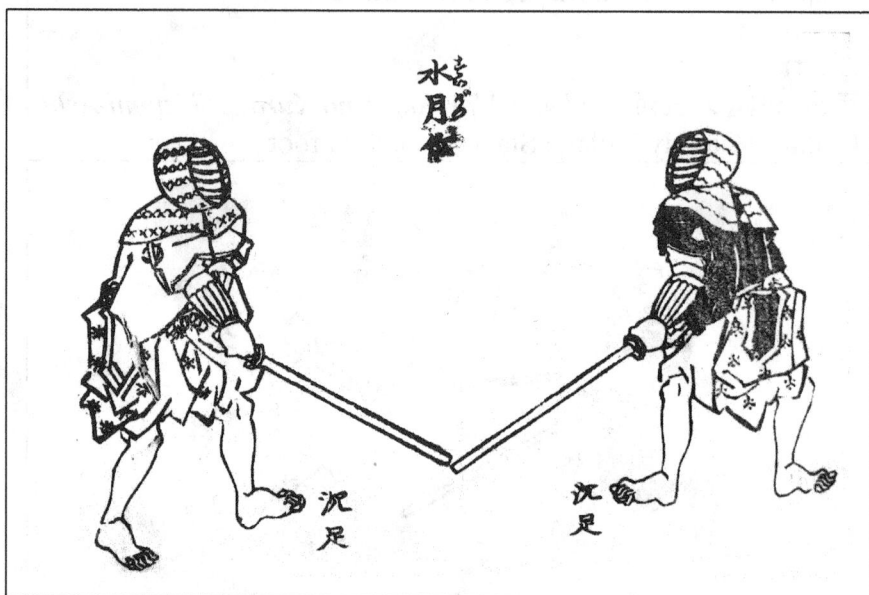

水月の位沈足 *Suigetsu no Kurai : Shizumu-Ashi*
Clear-eyed Stance : Planted Foot

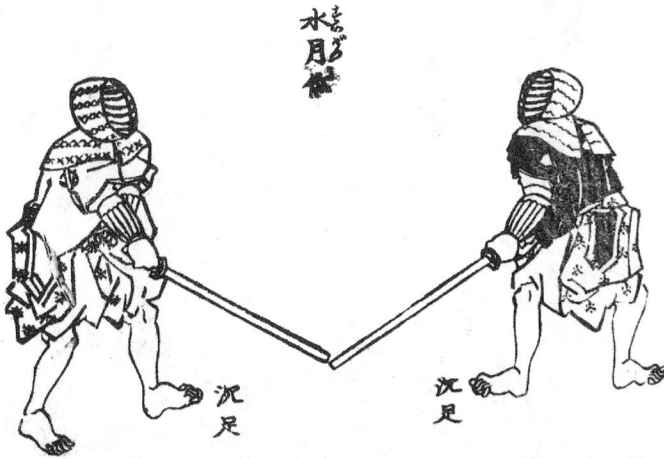

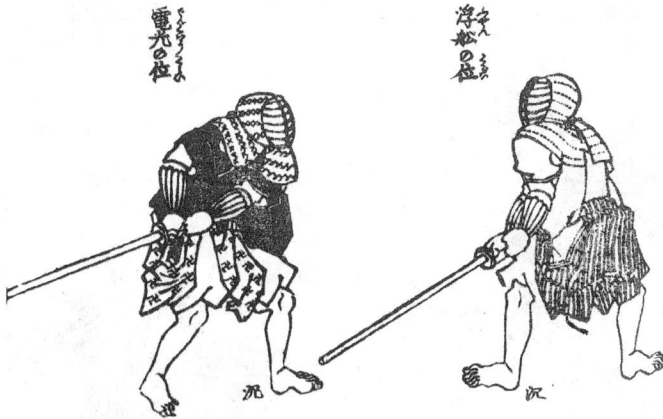

(Left)
電光の位沈足 *Denko no Kurai : Shizumu-Ashi*
Lightning Bolt Stance : Planted Foot

(Right)
浮船の位沈足 *Fusen no Kurai : Shizumu-Ashi*
Floating Boat Stance : Planted Foot

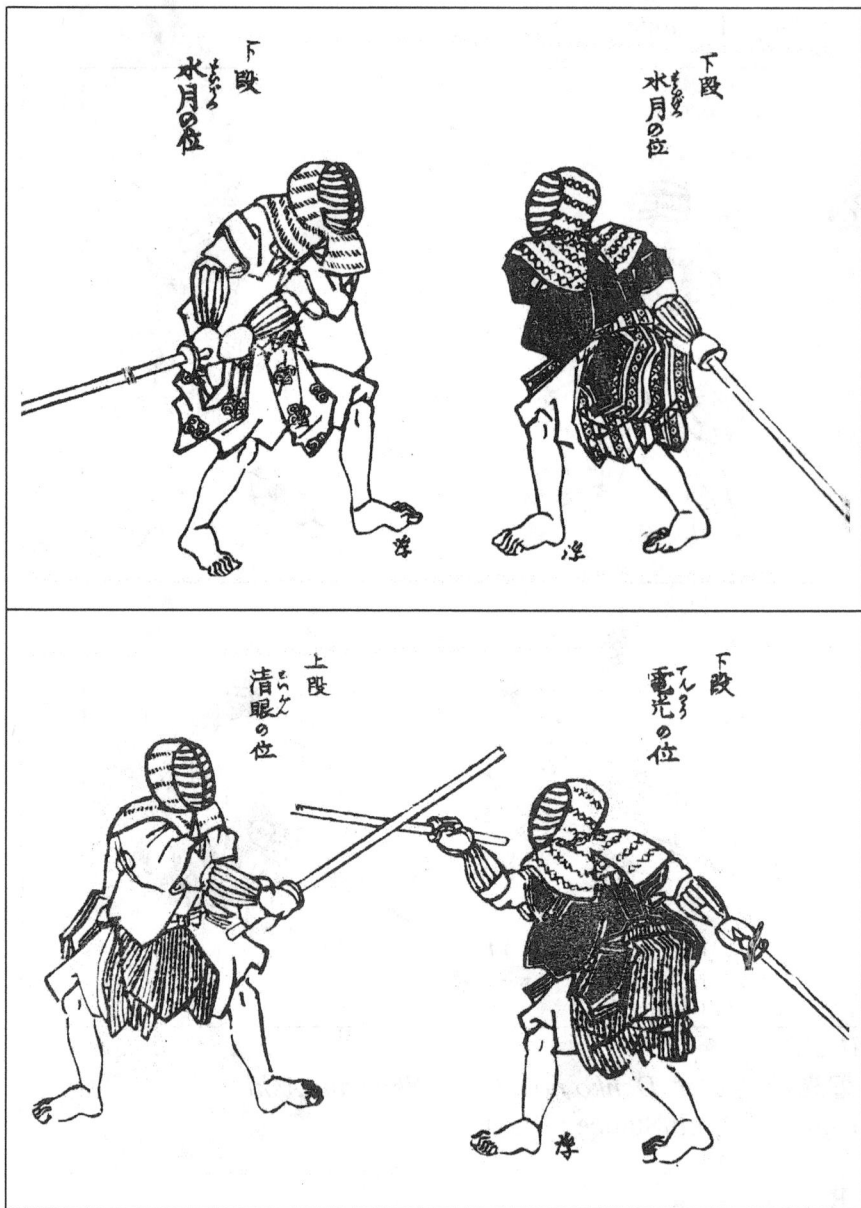

(Left) 下段　水月の位 浮 *Gedan : Suigetsu no Kurai : Uki-Ashi*
Gedan : Moon Reflected on Water Stance: Floating foot

(Right)
下段　水月の位 浮 *Gedan : Suigetsu no Kurai : Uki-Ashi* Gedan :
Moon Reflected on Water Stance : Floating foot

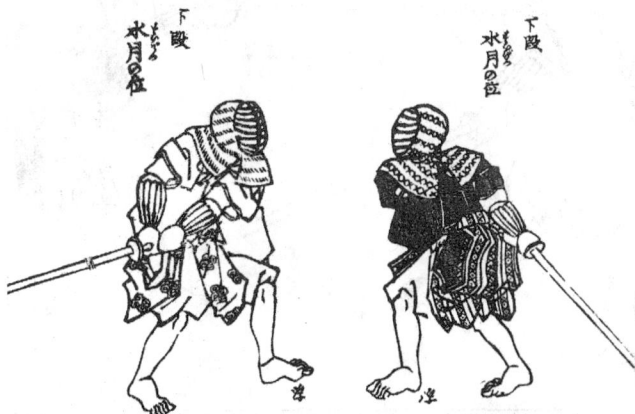

(Left)
下段　電光の位浮 *Gedan : Denko no Kurai : Uki-Ashi*
Gedan : Lightning Stance : Floating foot

(Right)
下段　清眼の位浮 *Gedan : Seigan no Kurai : Uki-Ashi*
Gedan : Clear-eyed : Floating foot

Jodan : Seigan no Kurai : Uki-Ashi
Jodan : Clear-eyed Stance : Floating foot

Here you are meant to keep your eye on the end of the opponent's Tachi while at the same time keep your other eye on the eight directions around you.

下段睡猫の位沈足 *Gedan : Suibyo no Kurai : Shizumu Ashi*

Gedan : Sleeping Cat Stance : Planted foot

Explanation is the same as before

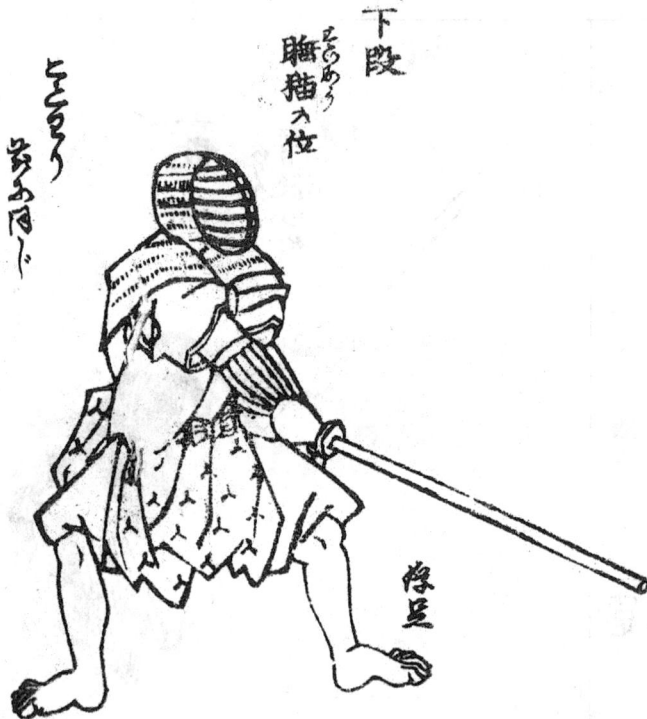

下段
睡猫の位
ことわりまへにあり

寒夜聞霧の位 浮足 *Kanyashimo wo Kiku no Kurai : Uki Ashi*
The stance of being able to hear frost crack on a winter's night :
Floating foot

寒夜聞霧の位　浮足

入引の位浮足 *Nyuin no Kurai : Ukiashi*
Moving in and Out : Floating Foot

The explanation for this is the same as for Denko no Kurai.

ことわり電光の位に具に書くしるし侯也

入引の位　浮足

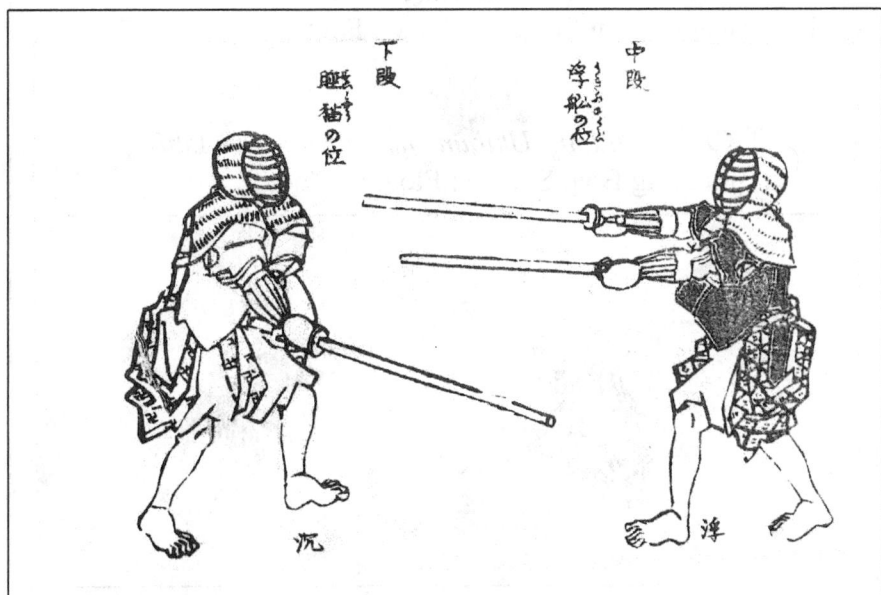

(Left)
下段 睡猫 *Gedan : Suibyo no Kurai Shizumu-Ashi*
Gedan : Sleeping Cat Stance : Planted Foot

(Right)
中段浮船の位 *Chudan : Ukibune no Kurai : Uki-Ashi*
Chudan : Floating Boat Stance : Floating Foot

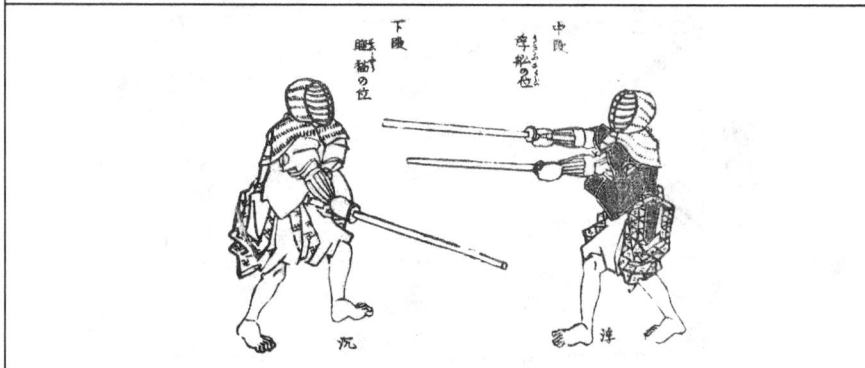

(Left)
中段浮船の位 *Chudan : Ukibune no Kurai : Uki-Ashi*
Chudan : Floating Boat Stance : Floating Foot

(Right)
上段寒夜聞霧の位
Jodan : Kanyashimo wo Kiku no Kurai : Uki-Ashi
The stance of being able to hear frost crack on a winter's night :
Floating Foot

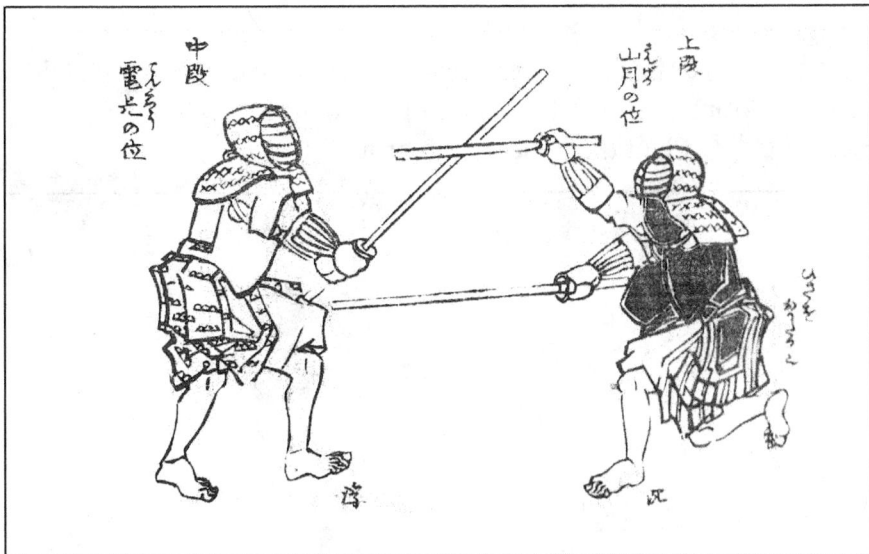

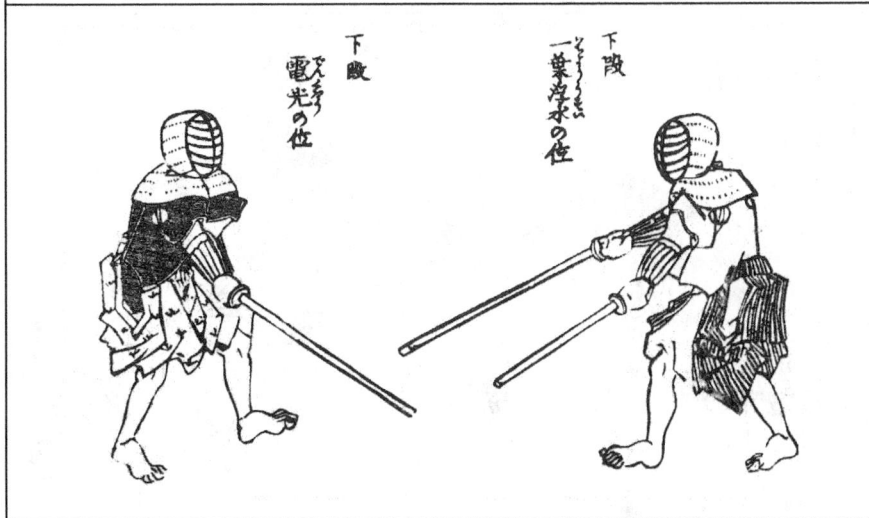

(Left)

中段電光の位浮き *Chudan : Denko no Kurai : Uki-Ashi*

Chudan : Lightning Bolt Stance : Floating Foot

(Right)

上段　山月の位沈 *Jodan : Yamatsuki no Kurai : Shizumu-Ashi*

Jodan : Mountain Moon Stance : Planted Foot.

膝を付ける Plant the knee on the ground.

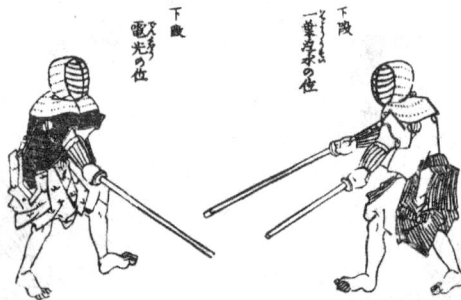

(Left)

下段電光の位 *Gedan : Denko no Kurai*

Gedan : Lightning Bolt Stance

(Right)

下段一葉浮水の位 *Gedan : Ichiefusui no Kurai*

Gedan: Leaf floating upon water Stance

(Left and right) 浮 Uki- Ashi : Floating foot
Note: The round ball on the end of the spear is padding for training.

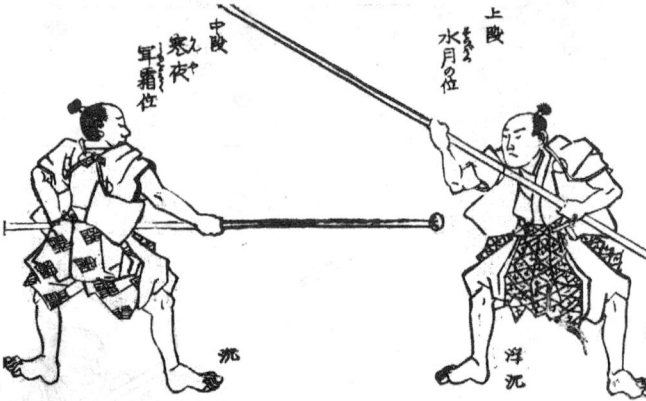

(Left)
中段　寒夜聞霧の位沈
Chudan : Kanyasimowokiku no Kurai : Shizumu-Ashi
Chudan : The stance of being able to hear frost crack on a winter's night : Planted foot

(Right) 上段水月の位　浮沈
Jodan Suigetsu no Kurai Uki-Shizumu Ashi
Jodan : Moon Reflected on Water Stance : Floating/planted foot

Left)
上段 電光の位下段 浮沈
Jodan: Denko no Kurai : Uki-Shizumu Ashi
Jodan : Lightning Bolt Stance : Floating/Planted foot

(Right)
村雲の位　沈 *Murakumo no Kurai : Shizumu-Ashi*
Cloudy Village : Planted foot

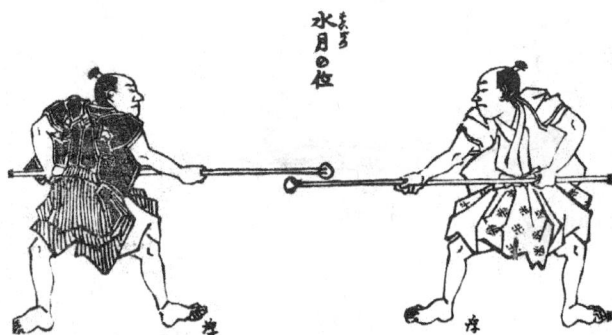

(Left and Right) 水月の位　浮 *Suigetsu no Kurai : Uki-Ashi*
Moon Reflected on Water Stance : Floating foot

(Left)

下段電光の位沈 *Gedan : Denko no Kurai : Shizumu-Ashi*

Gedan : Lightning Bolt Stance : Planted foot

(Right)

中段清眼の位沈 *Chudan : Seigan no Kurai : Shizumu-Ashi*

Chudan : Clear-eyed Stance : Planted foot

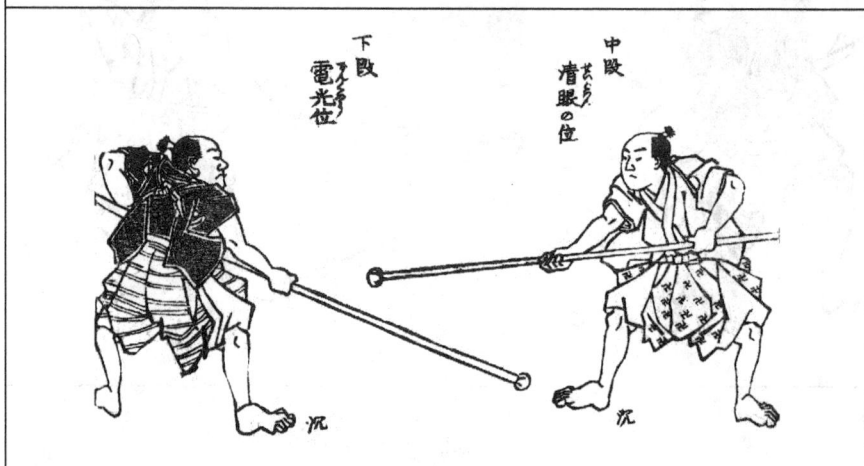

(Left and Right)下段電光の位沈 Gedan : Denko no Kurai :
Shizumu-Ashi

Gedan : Lightning Bolt Stance : Planted foot

(Left)

上段寒夜聞霧の位 沈
Kanyashimowokiku no Kurai Shizumu-Ashi
Jodan : The stance of being able to hear frost crack on a winter's night : Planted foot

(Right) 上段電光の位沈 *Jodan: Denko no Kurai Shizumu-Ashi*
Jodan : Lightning Bolt Stance : Planted foot

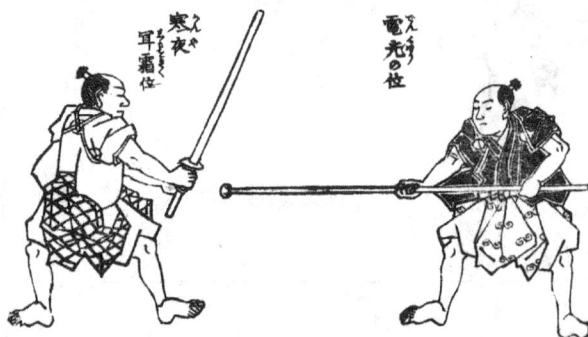

(Left)

上段 一葉浮水の位沉 Jodan *Ichiefusui no Kurai Shizumu-Ashi*
Jodan : Leaf floating upon water Stance : Planted Foot

(Right)

上段 電光の位沉 *Jodan Denko no Kurai : Shizumu-Ashi*
Jodan : Lightning Bolt Stance : Planted foot.

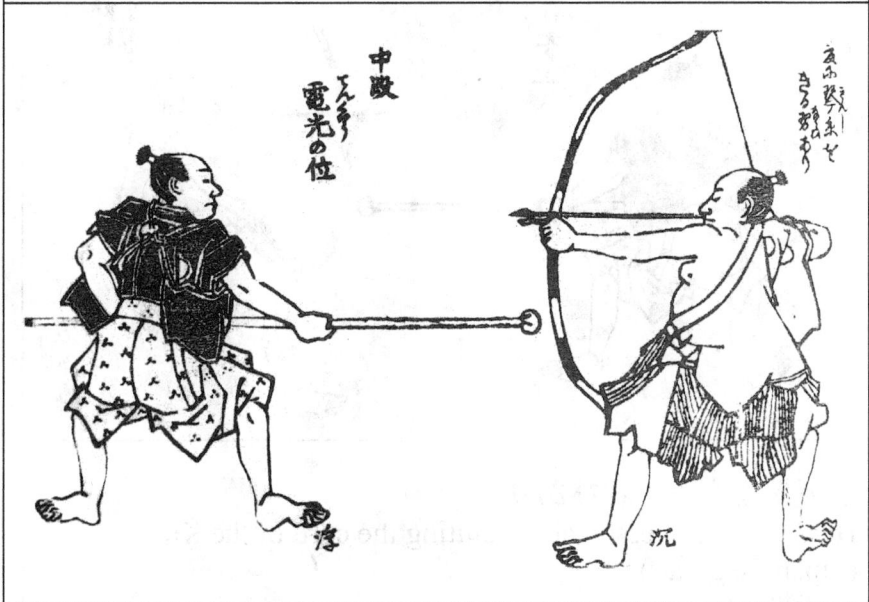

水月の位　*Suigetsu no Kurai*
Moon Reflected on Water Stance

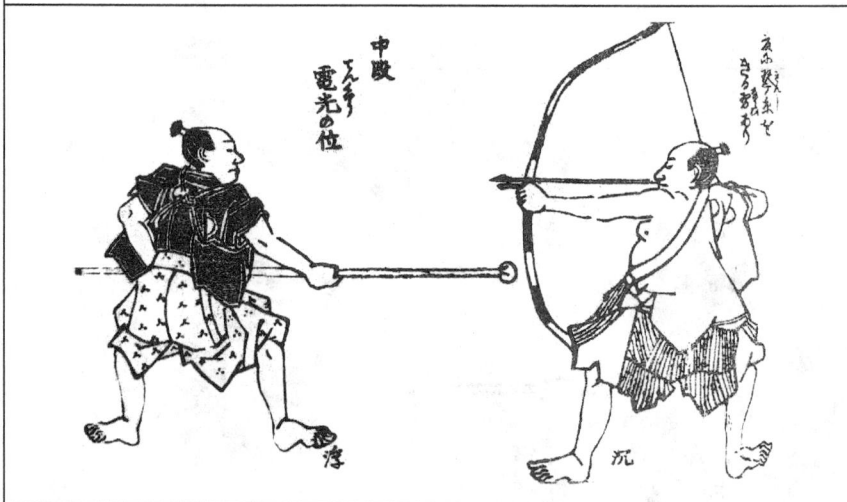

爰琴糸をきる　習ひあり
Here there is a lesson about cutting the cord of the Koto
(Japanese guitar)
(Left)
中段電光の位沉　Chudan : Denko no Kurai : Shizumu-Ashi
Chudan : Lightning Bolt Stance : Planted foot

手留 *Tedome* : Stopping the Hand

乱勝 *Rankatsu* : Riotous Victory

雲切 *Kumokiri* : Cutting the Cloud

雷光 *Raiko* : Lightning

鈎極　*Kokyoku* (Extreme Hook)

Translator's Note:

The final five images show a human figure training with different types of Tengu, Japanese mountain goblins. The Tengu are associated with trickery an mischief, though they also are known to teach martial arts, particularly sword to certain people. This seems to show Yoshitsune learning sword fighting from various types of Tengu. While there is no information regarding the meaning of these techniques there are other historical documents that show human figures fighting Tengu.

The first book is an Aisu Kage School Scroll from 1576. The illustration on the left is from and the image on the right is from the Kage School document.

Kendo Solo Training	Aisu Kage Scroll (1576)

This and the following page contain more comparisons to the Kage School scroll. The positioning is very similar however the Kage School scroll shows the point you cut, and the arm (or leg) of the beast having been cut off.

Aisu Kage School Scroll (1576)

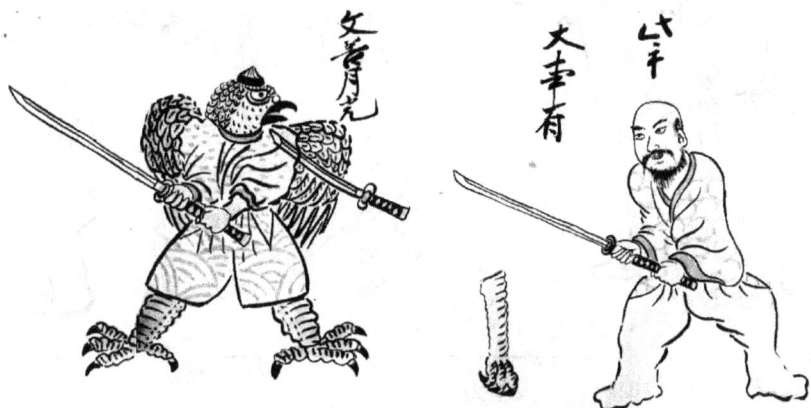

Solo Kendo Training

Aisu Kage School Scroll (1576)

Solo Kendo Training

Another book that features Tengu is an undated, but probably Edo Era scroll, called Kenpo-zu, *Illustrations of Fighting.* This scroll shows both combatants as different types of Tengu.

Illustrations of Fighting (Edo Era)

Solo Kendo Training
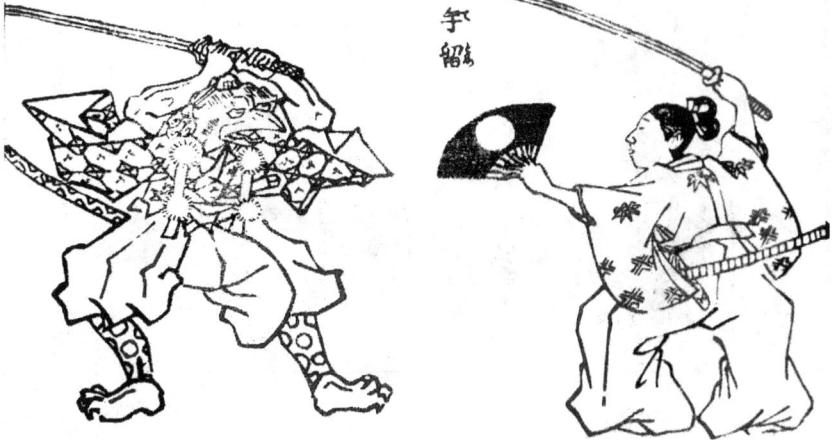

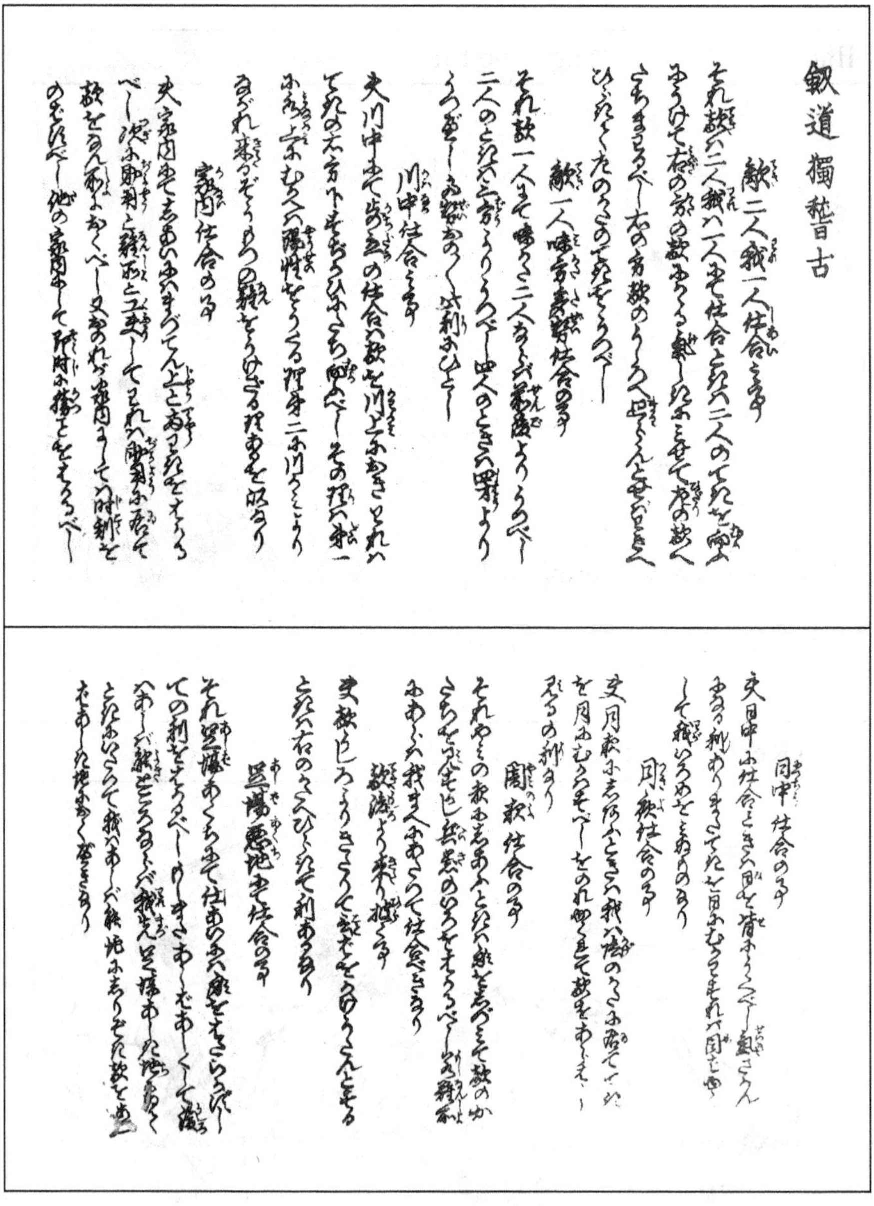

劔道獨稽古

敵二人我一人仕合の事

川中仕合の事

家間仕合の事

闇夜仕合の事

夜月夜仕合の事

晝博奕池仕合の事

敵二人、我一人試合の事
Teki Futari, Ware Hitori Shiai no Koto
When You Are Alone Against Two Attackers

The learning of Kenjutsu and Jujutsu are by the order of the lord however all other study should be devoted to keeping yourself on the true path and preserving your integrity. This is very important. When you are alone and facing two opponents, position yourself so you are standing opposite both of them. Give the impression that you are going to attack the opponent on your right, then join combat with the enemy on your left.

敵一人、味方多数試合の事
Teki Hitori, Mikata Tasu Shiai no Koto
Fighting Against One Person With Many Soldiers

If there is but a single enemy soldier and two of your warriors, one of you should attack from behind. If there are three of you then strike in from three different directions. If there are four of you attack from four different directions. For greater numbers follow this same principal.

川中試合の事
Kawanaka Shiai no Koto
Fighting in the Middle of a River

When fighting a battle in a river you should position your forces so that the enemy is upstream from you. You should be on the right hand side, diagonally opposite the enemy. The underlying theory here is, first of all, if you are facing the flow of the river you can receive the Yosei 陽性, or combined energy of the opponent and the river. Second, scraps of wood and so forth that flow down from upstream will not cause a damage to your forces.

If during the afternoon the sunlight should be to your back. If you are armed with Yari 鑓, or spears, then your forces should be placed at the Mizu-giwa 水際, or where the water meets the land. They should strike from Gedan Kamae. This will help to conserve your energy.

家内試合の事
Kanai Shiai no Koto
Fighting in a House

Should you ever have to join combat within a house you should first gauge the height of the ceiling as well as the distance to the walls on your right and left. Next, you should consider your Joyo 助用 or the spot which is the most advantageous for you, in addition to your Nansho 難所, or your weak point in the room. Devise a Kufu, or device, that will allow you to be set up in the beneficial Joyo position. At the same time the enemy should be forced into the most difficult position, the Nansho.

Further, if you are within your own home try to delay the confrontation as much as possible. Should you be in a dwelling not your own then try to end the confrontation as quickly as possible.

日中試合の事
Nicchu Shiai no Koto
Fighting During Midday

When fighting during the day be sure to have the sun at your back. You will receive a beneficial push of Ki 気 or spirit. Further, the sun will be bright in the enemy's eyes and they will not be able to read the faces of your men.

月夜試合の事
Tukiyo Shiai no Koto
Fighting on a Moonlit Night

When fighting at night under a moon lit sky, you should place your forces in the shadow and the moonlight in the enemy's face. The benefit is that you will be hidden and the faces of the enemy will be clearly illuminated.

闇夜試合の事
Yamiyo Shiai no Koto
Fighting on a Dark Night

When battling on a dark night drop your body down low and concentrate on the formation the enemy has taken and try to determine how they are armed. Note however that should the terrain not be to your advantage you should move in and engage the enemy. It can be beneficial to conceal your forces in a dark place in order to spy on the enemy.

敵が後方から来た時、披く事
Teki ga Koho Kara Kita Toki, Hiraku Koto
Opening up When Attacked From Behind

If an enemy approaches from behind and calls out to you as he cuts in, the best defense is to move out to the right. This will all be to the enemy's disadvantage.

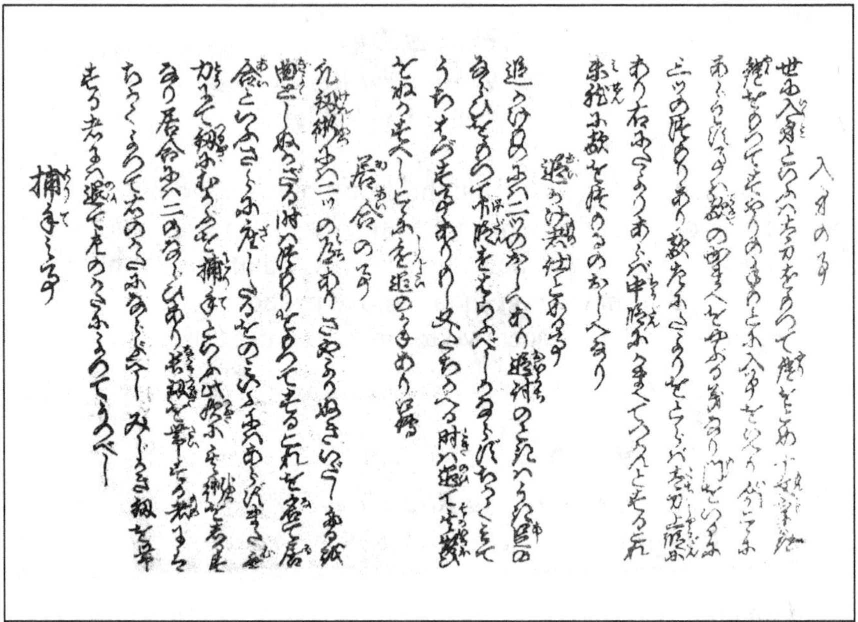

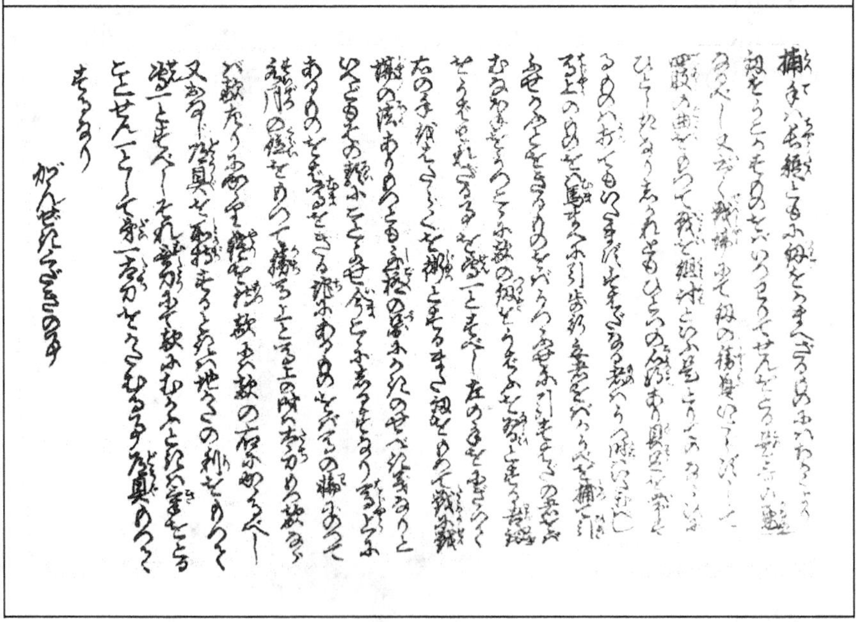

にゅうしん
入身の事
Nyushin no Koto
Entering With Your Body

Generally the meaning of the term Nyushin 入身 is to stop the movement of the Yari with the Tachi. You can also use a Juji-Kagi Yari, or a hooked cross shaped headed spear, to catch the opponent's spear and enter Temoto 手元, where the opponent's hands hold the spear. What is written here is a method for breaking the opponent's Kamae, or stance.

There are three ways of thinking for those entering the gate, which is another way of saying entering deep into the enemy's space. If you detect the Kehai 気配, or the intention, of the opponent you should take Daijodan no Kamae. Should you detect the enemy's Keihai coming from the right, you should go into Chudan Kamae while visualizing doing a Tsuki 突, or straight thrust. When you sense Keihai in front of you enter while staying aware the space near you and farther away as well. This is the best method for detecting the Keihai of the enemy.

おいかけもの し と
追駆者仕留める事
Oikake Mono no Shitomere Koto
How to Strike Down an Escaping Samurai

With regards to pursuing a fleeing soldier there are two things taught. When striking while pursuing you should make use of techniques that have Uki-ashi and strike with a sweeping Gedan cut to the lower part of the body. You should take care with your distancing as though it seems you are close enough, you may end up missing your target entirely.

Should the enemy come about you should, initially, drop back a step thereby lessoning the opponent's energy. Here you are required to evaluate the relative distance near or far to the opponent. There is a Kuden.

いあい
居合の事
Iai no Koto
Sword Drawing

This section will have to be balanced with what was written in the previous chapters. This is the thing that has been given the name Iai. However, Iai is not done exclusively from a seated position. It can also refer to when you take down an opponent armed with a sword when you are Muto, or without a sword. Next that technique will be explained.

There are two techniques in Iai. For opponents with a long sword in their belt, close in until you are aligned with their right shoulder. For opponents with a short sword, you should drop back and cut in toward the opponent's right shoulder.

とりて
捕手の事
Torite no Koto
Unarmed Fighting

Torite refers to when you are fighting without any sort of blade, long or short and you are against a person swinging a sword. You deceive this person and take the advantage with your Ashi Sabaki, or footwork, along with three main points. These will be briefly detailed below. Abbreviated below.

On the battlefield, when the swords do not end the fight, battling on with feet and hands is called Kumi Uchi. These are the same methods as the Torite Techniques. That being said there is a single way of thinking with regards to these. A person wearing Tabi will not injure his feet, a barefoot person will hurt his feet.

A mounted rider should be pulled from his horse while a foot soldier should be grabbed by the head and pulled down onto his back. A helmeted warrior should be pulled facedown. A shirtless many should be struck in the chest and the most important thing is to take the enemy's sword. Further, take great care that your own blade is not stolen away. This is a technique that holds or wraps up with the left hand while the right does the action.

In addition, there is a way to fight whilst holding a sword. Typically an illustration of this extreme situation should be placed here in my opinion but as it is the same I will just write a description. For a warrior on horseback, cut at the horse. For a man on the ground, trace a circle around him on your horseback and win with Suigetsu no Kurai.

For situations where both are mounted on horseback. If the opponent is holding a Tachi, attack from the opponents left. An opponent holding a spear should be met on the right. These attacking methods are essential.

Further, in the case where you are both armed with the same weapon, it is important to make use of Chi no Ri, or the advantage of the terrain, to your best advantage. In addition, when Muto, or without a sword, and facing off against an enemy the most important thing is Kisen wo Sei Suru 機先を制する, or take the advantage by striking first in an unexpected manner. From there you should next completely block the movement of the enemy's sword and take his weapon away from him.

がんせきくだきの事
Gansekikudaki no Koto
Crushing a Great Rock

The weighted portion of this is formed from a hundred Monme 匁, or 375 grams, of lead. Form it into a ball and cover it with skin. Sew up the seam where the two ends of the hide overlap and attach a short cord. An opponent can be struck between the eyebrows from between two and three Ken, or 3.6 to 5.4 meters/yards away. In the summer or other warmer times striking the chest bone will immediately cause a man to crumple.

	この土は 袂_{たもと} に入れて持ち運ぶ事 You should place this ball in your Tamoto 袂, or sleeve, and carry it about with you.

(Written inside the circle) You should place this ball in your Tamoto 袂, or sleeve, and carry it about with you.

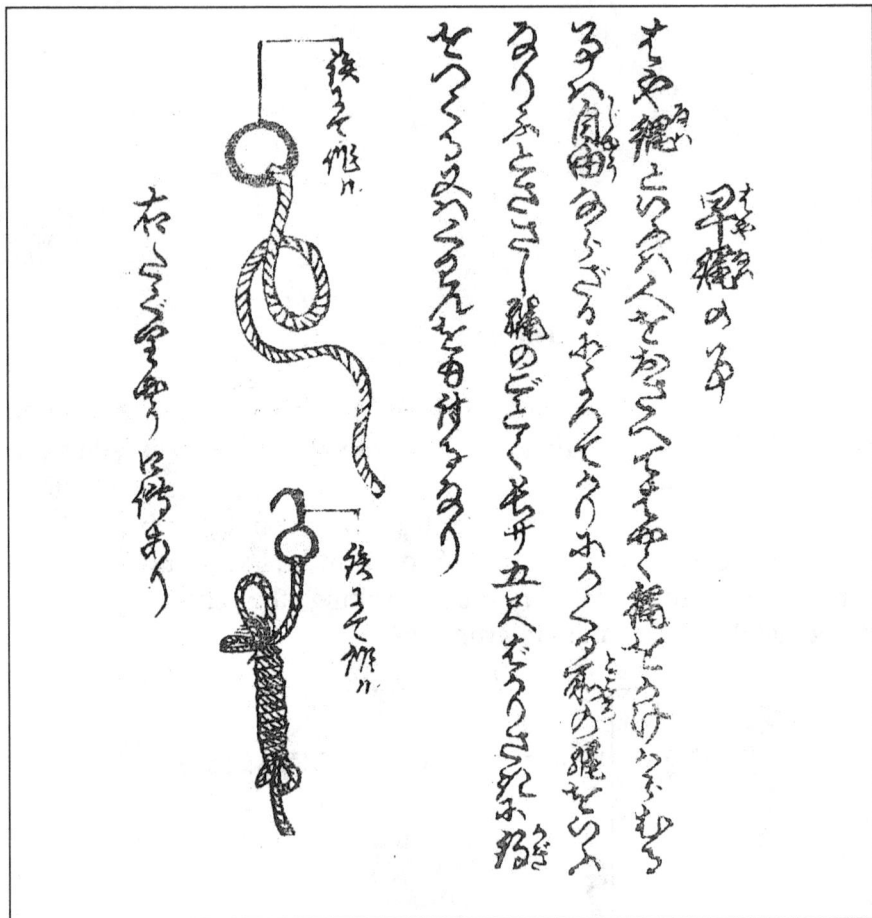

はやなわ
早縄の事
Hayanawa no Koto
Fast Tie Binding

Hayanawa refers to a method for quickly restraining a person by rapidly tying them up with rope. Typically a long thick rope of Five Shaku, or 1.5 meters is used. On the end of that a hook is attached. A ring is also sometimes used.

There is a Kuden related bringing the rope in to the right.

Note : The arrows all say, "This part is made of iron."

92

取籠者に心得すること
Torikomori Mono ni Kokoroe suru Koto
How to Handle a Samurai You Have Surrounded

If you have surrounded a person, the first thing you should do in find out who they are. If the person is a Bushi, or Samurai, they will become stronger as time passes. If it is a person of lower status however they will become weaker as time passes.

剣術虚実の事
Kenjutsu Kyojitsu no Koto
Using Truth and Falsehood With the Sword

For the most part within Kenjutsu, the sword arts, the term Kyo-Jitsu, or Truth-Falsehood refer to showing that you are going to cut in from Jodan when you actually are going to cut from Gedan. Show that you are going to cut from Gedan and then cut in from Chudan. It is of the upmost importance to keep this concept in mind as you go into Kamae with the Tachi.

For an opponent that enters quickly, you should open up to one side and strike. For an opponent that attacks slowly it is best to go into Chudan. That being said it is important to watch the opponent's eyes.

A person whose eyes are red (signifying a person who is wound up) should be handled calmly. However a person whose eyes are white (a brave warrior) should be dealt with using sudden violent attacks.

柔術、当身の事
Jujutsu Atemi no Koto
On the Subject of Jujutsu and Atemi, or Striking

For the most part Jujutsu refers to using a joint lock on the opponent's feet or legs. Further, Atemi striking refers to striking the chest or the area under the armpits. Also striking between the eyes. Below that are points like Kage no Fu, the solar plexus, which if struck is something that cannot be endured.

眼潰しの事
Metsubushi no Koto
On the Topic of Metsubushi, Blinding powders

Open a small hole in an egg's shell. Blow out the contents and fill it with powdered Togarashi, or red pepper, and cover the hole with paper. Then put it in your Tamoto, or end of the sleeve of your Kimono. When you are faced with an enemy smash it on their face. Also you can bury a poisonous Mamushi snake in the ground and pile horse manure on top. Add finely chopped grass and mix it. After powdering it, roll it in paper tissue like you would use to wipe your nose. Blowing it at an opponent will cause them to lose consciousness. This method is rather incomplete and has not been fully tested. You should probably rely more on the teachings of your master and not attempt it without his permission. This is but an extract of the Record of Military Strategy left to us by Yamamoto Kansuke.

In the end it is essential to understand that both Kenjutsu and Jujutsu are not only to protect the life of your lord but are tools with which you can protect yourself and keep yourself on the correct path. Despite knowing Kenjutsu it is best to err on the side of caution and not enter a mountain road infested with brigands. There is a saying that goes "A little bit of military training can be the cause of great injury."

敵顔色顔持見る事
Teki Kao Iro Kao Mochi Miru Koto
Observing the Enemy's Face

It is important to look at the face of your enemy when you are set to engage in a Kiri-Ai 斬り合い or a sword fight. If the face has become red then the enemy is not in their right mind. As they have become unstrung it is not necessary to resort to a Kufu. Their spirit is not settled.

Next, if the face is pale it is evidence of a person who is fearful. When a person is fearful they value their life greatly and are unlikely to strike first. Such a person is not thinking about winning, only of escaping.

Further, in order to gain an advantage by judging the enemy's face, know that when the opponent is looking up he is observing something in the distance. When looking downward he is observing something nearby. It is important not to Yudan 油断, or become careless or miscalculate here.

A closer look at The Sword Scroll: Volume 2
An Illustrated Guide to Kendo Solo Training
End